Managing Family Meltdown

of related interest

First Steps in Intervention with Your Child with Autism
Frameworks for Communication
Phil Christie, Elizabeth Newson, Wendy Prevezer and Susie Chandler
Illustrated by Pamela Venus
ISBN 978 1 84905 011 1

Hints and Tips for Helping Children with Autism Spectrum Disorders
Useful Strategies for Home, School, and the Community
Dion E. Betts and Nancy J. Patrick
ISBN 978 1 84310 896 2

The Red Beast
Controlling Anger in Children with Asperger's Syndrome
K.I. Al-Ghani
ISBN 978 1 84310 943 3

Coach Yourself Through the Autism Spectrum
Ruth Knott Schroeder
Foreword by Linda Miller
ISBN 978 1 84905 801 8

Managing Family Meltdown

The **Low Arousal Approach** and **Autism**

Linda Woodcock and Andrea Page

Illustrated by Chris Woodcock
Foreword by Andrew McDonnell

Jessica Kingsley Publishers
London and Philadelphia

First published in 2010
by Jessica Kingsley Publishers
116 Pentonville Road
London N1 9JB, UK
and
400 Market Street, Suite 400
Philadelphia, PA 19106, USA

www.jkp.com

Library of Congress Cataloging in Publication Data
Woodcock, Linda.
 Managing family meltdown : the low arousal approach and autism / Linda Woodcock
and Andrea Page ; foreword by Andrew McDonnell ; illustrated by Chris Woodcock.
   p. cm.
 Includes bibliographical references and index.
 ISBN 978-1-84905-009-8 (pb : alk. paper) 1. Parents of children with disabilities-
-Psychology. 2. Parents of autistic children--Psychology. 3. Autistic children--Family
relationships. 4. Autism in children. I. Page, Andrea. II. Title.
 HQ759.913.W66 2010
 649'.154--dc22

                              2009027019

British Library Cataloguing in Publication Data
A CIP catalogue record for this book is available from the British Library

ISBN 978 1 84905 009 8

Printed and bound in the United States by
Thomson-Shore, 7300 Joy Road, Dexter, MI 48130

Contents

Acknowledgements

Linda would like to thank the following:

All those people who at varying stages accompanied me on this journey. All my colleagues at autism.west midlands, especially Sue Hatton, without whom we would not have been able to develop this work, thanks for your support and friendship. To Andy and everyone at Studio III for believing in the importance of working with families. All the families I have worked with over the years, you taught me so much. Special thanks to Andrea, it's been great working together and finally to my FAB husband Chris and our beautiful boy Christopher, our journey goes on and where ever it takes us, I couldn't ask for better travelling companions.

Andrea would like to thank the following:

Like Linda, it is the families that I met over the years as a community nurse who have influenced me, who I would like to send a thank you to first. Gerri and my colleagues within the clinical skills team at Birmingham City University, my husband Sean and daughter Alex also deserve a thank you (especially for the coffees). Working with Linda has been fantastic…it was a delight to meet someone and get on so well right from the start!

Foreword

It is a privilege to be asked to write a foreword for such a practical book. In my view, any materials which can help to provide some support, especially to family members who may be experiencing directly or indirectly challenging behaviours, should be strongly supported.

I have worked in this field for over 20 years as a practising clinical psychologist. It has always been very important for me to provide practical help and advice for carers. The vast majority of this work has tended to focus on residential services or schools. Support for families has always been an area that, for me, has been relatively neglected. Families often represent a 'silent majority' of people who are sometimes viewed by professionals as 'over involved' or troublesome. They often spend huge amounts of time with their relatives and we know that family members are often exposed to the same challenges as other carers in residential services.

I must also admit to several personal connections with this book. First, both of the authors are of course very well known to me and have a keen interest in providing support and training to families who have sons and daughters with autism and/or intellectual disabilities. In the case of Linda Woodcock, she combines both a professional perspective and the experiences of a mother of a young man with autism. Linda helped to develop training for families in behaviour management adapted from the Studio III approach. She is now also a lead trainer for my own organization – Studio III Training Systems. Linda delivers training and practical support sessions to families not just in the UK but also in Northern and Southern Ireland, Denmark and South Africa. The demand for her type of work is huge and my colleagues and I are happy to support these projects as we have clearly witnessed the benefits of this approach with families.

Andrea Page is an experienced nurse practitioner who also shares a passionate interest in training and support for families who have children and adults who present with challenging behaviours. Andrea was involved in a pioneering approach, training family members in behaviour management strategies (Shinnick and McDonnell 2003) which also included some physical interventions which were very much regarded as a taboo subject at the time. I remember a senior health service manager saying to me at the time 'You can't teach those methods to families as we cannot guarantee that they will not abuse the methods.' My own response was very clear as I believe strongly that we need to provide family members with a range of supports; in some cases this will include physical interventions. In sum, if training in these methods is appropriate for care staff then they should also be appropriate for families.

The second area of involvement is that I have helped to develop the low arousal approach to managing challenging behaviours. This approach is clearly a cornerstone of this book and it is especially pleasing to see the ideas becoming increasingly more popular over the years. In the early 1990s, I became a little disillusioned with the lack of practical advice and support about crisis management strategies that was available to staff. For me, managing behaviour in the short term was a necessary first step for carers before attempts could be made to change these behaviours in the long term. In addition I found that the more confident that carers became in managing these behaviours, the more likely they were to take risks and empower people. I first published an article using the term over 15 years ago as a collection of crisis management strategies (McDonnell, McEvoy and Dearden 1994). Since this time the ideas have become much more sophisticated. The low arousal approach was for me a reflective approach to crisis management which has made me ask a number of simple questions.

1. What is my own contribution to the challenging behaviour? Most importantly, if I sometimes make behaviours worse by what I do or say, then I can also make them less likely to occur. This is a very positive message as carers need to reflect on their practice and learn from their mistakes and successes.

2. When should we reduce demands and requests? In my work, I still see extremely stressed service users in highly stressed environments, usually with stressed family members. Asking carers to take their foot off an accelerator pedal and reduce stress is not always easy to do. But, in reality, stress reduction is a critical component of all support plans that aim to manage challenging behaviours. This also means that stress reduction is individual in nature. I remember working with an adult with severe learning disabilities and autism who attended weekly Snoezelen sessions. He liked rock music (which clearly relaxed him) but in

the sensory room, staff only offered him gentle music. It took a considerable period of time to convince staff that he did find loud music relaxing. (If anyone has experienced teenagers' music preferences they will know exactly what I mean!)

3. How do I prevent situations from reoccurring? There is a great deal of published work which focuses on person centred approaches. The advent of Positive Behaviour Supports (see Carr *et al.* 1999) has made constructive approaches more popular. In school settings, instead of thinking that a child has to learn to do 'X' or 'Y', it is better to think about what situations optimize learning. Creating environments which take account of physiological arousal and sensory issues is also a great challenge to service providers. I still witness individuals with many sensory triggers to their challenging behaviours being exposed to highly stressful group based situations. Family members should be presented with information which will help them lobby for high quality environments for their sons and daughters. Increasingly, home based packages of support are becoming more preferred options in the UK. Working in partnership with families is clearly an effective option when it works well.

This book is written for family members in a practical and, at times, blunt manner. In the introduction the authors clearly state their aims: 'This is a practical, honest, no nonsense handbook which we hope will give you the confidence, skills and knowledge to manage challenging behaviours.' I would think of this book as a guide with numerous illustrative examples.

The use of 'personal stories' enhances the approach, although I do acknowledge that every person is an individual, so that the strategies that work for one person will not always work for another. Even with this caveat, this book is full of 'real life' examples that are a joy to read and thought provoking.

Chapter 1 is an enlightening and very personal overview of autism. It combines everyday views about social under-standing, social communication and imagination and of course some of the most common theories such as theory of mind. In addition there is an emphasis on sensory issues and how they might relate to challenging or distressing situations. Similarly, the section on movement differences is both novel and prag-matic in nature. The practical case examples should really help family members. The material helps to provide the reader with an 'autism informed' approach to these issues. There is a real sense that understanding autism is a major part of the battle in managing very distressing behaviours. The authors in my view correctly conclude that 'the experience of children with ASD is at times frightening, bewildering and confusing; is it any wonder therefore that they often react with behaviours that we find challenging?'.

For me, practical knowledge about autism is very different from the classroom facts and figures that many professionals describe. The reality for many people with autism is that they may well experience extreme states of panic in what you or I would consider to be an everyday social situation.

Developing this theme, Chapter 2 contains a range of presenting issues for families training from self-injurious behaviours to sleep difficulties. The key to this chapter is in the title: 'Understanding challenging or distressed behaviour'. Understanding why someone behaves in the way they do can often lead to changes in perceptions of behaviour. I think it is especially important that the chapter starts with a tolerance exercise that is very familiar to my colleagues at Studio III. The message is clear and simple: if a person understands their own triggers they may be able to change them. I also like the fact that the authors resist the temptation to simply list numerous causes of challenging behaviour in a theoretical manner without addressing what to do about them. In my work I often encounter individuals who have a fantastic theoretical knowledge about challenging behaviours, but fail to put it into practice. There are sensible suggestions provided in this chapter which I am sure carers will find of use.

In Chapter 3 the 'low arousal way' is described in some detail. The advice again focuses on the practicalities of what a person should do in situations when they are confronted by a distressed individual. There is sensible advice provided by the authors about how to communicate with people within these situations. A practical example of this is that it has been long known that individuals who experience a state of 'hyperarousal' process information more slowly and in some cases actually 'tune out' to what a person is saying (McDonnell in press). The most common phrase I kept thinking about after reading the chapter was 'don't pour fuel on the fire'. I have numerous personal examples where I definitely have thrown fuel on the fire and I am certain that many readers will identify strongly with the idea that we do this inadvertently.

There is also an emphasis on our own beliefs and expectations about behaviour and how these can have a negative impact on families. This chapter contains common phrases that we hear people use, 'I shouldn't let them win.' Or 'I shouldn't let them get away with it.' The first published case study on low arousal approaches on an adult with intellectual disabilities in a care setting showed clear reductions in behavioural difficulties over an 18-month period (McDonnell, Reeves, Johnson and Lane 1998). Despite these gains, a small minority of staff did report that they felt that they were 'giving in' to the person far too much because they had reduced many of their daily demands and requests. Cognitive therapists have often stressed the need to focus on negative thoughts and beliefs in therapy (Beck 1975).

The use of video in Chapter 4 is a novel solution-focused approach. Again, many family members do not always require significant outside professional help to create useful behaviour management strategies. Using feedback from friends and supporters would appear to make a great deal of intuitive sense. Video is a powerful tool; it may also help families describe to professionals what difficulties they often experience. There are circumstances where video may not always be appropriate. I have worked with families who have unobtrusively videoed distressing behaviours of their sons and daughters. I must admit that this does make me feel somewhat uncomfortable. In Chapter 4 there is clearly a low key self-help theme which I would of course wholeheartedly support.

Chapter 5 stresses the need for dialogue in families. The emotional consequences of witnessing and participating in situations where an individual you love is extremely distressed are sometimes long term and damaging. This chapter really is a simple guide to getting families to 'debrief' after incidents. I also feel that professionals reading this chapter will be moved by the stories it contains. The low arousal approaches described in this book do involve carers taking 'a step backwards' in high risk situations. This may mean exposure to verbal and in some cases physical challenges for prolonged periods of time. Immediate debriefing may help families to cope with the emotional aftermath of such episodes. In addition their thoughts and underlying belief structures may be altered as a consequence of their experiences.

Chapter 6 provides a useful overview of medical approaches to the management of challenging behaviours. The authors very correctly point out the lack of evidence for some of these approaches. But, for a family member, basic help in demystifying some of the medications that are used to manage challenging behaviours should be a help. The experiences described by Linda Woodcock make sobering reading for any carer or professional. The practical advice provided in this chapter about managing hospital visits will be of great use. There are still concerns that this vulnerable group of individuals do not always get the best healthcare investigations. This is especially true if there is any kind of history of challenging behaviours.

Chapter 7 covers a range of common questions asked by family members. These range from individual questions about the diagnosis of autism to the important subjects of managing anger and the thorny issue of sexuality and relationships. The advice given by the authors avoids jargon and in keeping with the theme of this book is very pragmatic.

Finally, Chapter 8 provides yet more useful resources and advice about how carers should manage their own stress and look after their health. I particularly liked the idea of this chapter. In residential care settings staff are often replaced by new staff when they experience high levels of stress or 'burnout'. Many families often do not have the luxury to be replaced. I remember working with a family member who told me that she was far too busy to manage her stress. To manage stressful behaviours in others low arousal approaches require us to reflect about our own stress and the impact it has on other family members. I am reminded of the phrase by the poet John Donne: 'No man is an island entire of itself.' We all require some degree of support. To manage another person's behaviours requires a realistic assessment of our own basic needs.

In conclusion, I believe that practical books such as this are long overdue in the marketplace. It is my hope that many family members will not only read this material but will support others in the process. Although the title is 'Managing Family Meltdown' I believe the message is extremely positive. In most cases 'meltdowns' can be avoided and managed with simple low key, low arousal approaches. If this book empowers only a handful of families to manage these situations more positively then it will have achieved a great deal.

Andrew McDonnell, PhD, Clinical Psychologist,
Director of Studio III Training Systems

References

Beck, A.T. (1975) *Cognitive Therapy and the Emotional Disorders.* Madison: International Universities Press.

Carr, E.G., Horner, R.H., Turnbull, A.P., Marquis, J.G. et al. (1999) *Positive Behavior Support for People with Developmental Disabilities: A Research Synthesis.* Washington: AAMR.

McDonnell, A.A. (in press) *Managing Aggressive Behaviour in Care Environments: The Use of Low Arousal Approaches.* London: Wiley.

McDonnell, A.A., McEvoy, J. and Dearden, R.L. (1994) 'Coping with violent situations in the caring environment.' In T. Wykes (ed.) *Violence and Health Care Professionals.* London: Chapman and Hall, pp. 189–206.

McDonnell, A.A., Reeves, S., Johnson, A. and Lane, A. (1998) 'Management challenging behaviours in an adult with learning disabilities: the use of low arousal.' *Behavioural and Cognitive Psychotherapy 26,* 163–171.

Shinnick, A. and McDonnell, A.A. (2003) 'Training family members in behaviour management methods.' *Learning Disability Practice 6,* 2, 16–20.

Introduction:
Setting the Scene

Linda's voice

Winston Churchill famously said about the Soviet Union and its propensity for secrecy that it was a 'riddle wrapped inside a conundrum inside an enigma'. That is how I have come to see my son's autism – a secret that I need to discover and decipher. Coming to understand the many facets of his autism has become the biggest challenge of our lives as a family. It seems each day throws up another problem; the twists and turns he experiences as he tries to make sense of the world impact on us to the point where quite often we are left just as frightened and bewildered as he must be.

Christopher is a beautiful 21-year-old young man who can sing like a bird and loves nothing better than splashing about in the swimming pool. He also happens to have autism and a severe intellectual learning disability. Christopher finds our neurotypical world incredibly frightening and confusing; this fear, this confusion, makes him very anxious. These anxieties frequently make him very distressed. When he becomes distressed he is likely to injure himself and others around him. He is an incredibly complex young man; every day is a challenge for him and those who live and work with him. When we get it right the rewards are enormous; when we get it wrong the results can be disastrous.

The early years were dominated by his ability to keep going for what seemed 24 hours a day. He was like a tornado through our lives. He was, however, generally anxiety free and had an enormous capacity for enjoying whatever he found amusing. Living with Christopher was by turns exhausting and exhilarating.

When puberty hit Christopher it was like a locomotive out of control; it hit him full on. It was as if overnight he became a different child. Intellectually as a family we knew it would happen but we could not have been prepared for the impact this had on him; his mood oscillated between extreme anxiety and excitability to being incredibly distressed and tearful. It took all our inner reserves and it became increasingly difficult to keep Christopher on an even keel. His behaviour became more and more erratic and he began to hurt himself and us. We became more and more isolated as a family. We could no longer do all the family things we had previously managed to do. There were no services that could help us in any real way and so we coped alone. We sustained many injuries but worse than this Christopher was hurting himself; for us as a family the self-injury was far more painful to endure than anything he could inflict on us. It is impossible to convey the emotional impact that the distress and unhappiness Christopher was experiencing had on those that cared for him. This was an incredibly bleak period in our lives, which I hope will never be repeated.

It was obvious to us that he was struggling with an inner rage and fear and he would sometimes lash out at us and other times turn this rage in on himself. On one occasion which typified his behaviour Christopher had attacked me and had hold of my hair so tightly that it was pointless trying to free myself. He had been pulling me around the room and now pulled me toward the floor. He lunged at me with his mouth open and his teeth made contact with my shoulder. He suddenly let go of my hair and I rolled out of his way and curled my legs up and put my hands over my head. He was sobbing now as he threw himself onto the sofa and pulled his sweater over his head. He began to jab his elbow into his side. Every fibre of my body wanted to reach out and comfort him. Watching him pummel his flesh caused me far more pain than any bite. His sobs subsided and he said 'Cuddle mummy.' I sat down beside him and he put his head on my lap and I began to massage his head, singing softly his favourite lullaby: 'Hush little baby don't say a word, papa's gonna buy you a mocking bird.' I finished the song and he said 'Again.' I always had to repeat it at least twice. I continued to massage his head and sing quietly; the pummelling slowed down and eventually stopped. He stayed still for some time and then he suddenly jumped up laughing loudly shouting 'Cheeky monkey, cheeky monkey.' He stopped and put his fingers to the tears that were trickling slowly down my face; he grimaced and said 'Sad face, mummy laughing.' My beautiful boy was 13 years old.

When Christopher was diagnosed I did what most parents do, I contacted the organizations both nationally and locally that could give me information (pre-internet of course!). Looking back, the fact that I was in shock and going through the grieving process, it is not surprising that although I read the information the actual impact of his autism on his and our lives was not fully appreciated. I could eventually recite the triad of impairment and tell you which areas of his life would be affected, but I was for a long time unable to bridge the gap between my (rather limited) knowledge of the subject and applying that to Christopher's autism. I look now at the wealth of information available and the opportunities for accessing training and workshops and I realize just how little was available all those years ago. When during the teenage years, Christopher's autism became a major challenge to him and us it was our ability to revisit all the information and connect the two that saved us from complete meltdown. It became obvious to us why his behaviour was so challenging when we really began to realize how difficult it was for him to exist in what must have seemed to him like a very threatening and alien world. The behaviours he adopted although seemingly bizarre all began to make sense. We developed a new respect for these behaviours and started to question our own attitudes and thoughts. We did what Christopher was unable to do, that is we put ourselves in his position: we walked more than a mile in his shoes and it was a very uncomfortable journey. We started to view Christopher in a different light. We were able to see that the sometimes violent behaviour he displayed was not because he wanted to hurt us – it was just a very understandable reaction to fear and uncertainty – it was the autism getting in the way.

We had to go back to basics and virtually start again. This was the start of the second stage of our journey with Christopher and although it was probably the most traumatic and saddest time of our lives so far we as we continued to travel the rockiest road we had ever experienced, it was also the time when we learned the most about him and ourselves.

I had been working in the charity sector with family carers for several years although I avoided any jobs where autism was a focus until I was emotionally ready. By the time Christopher was 16 and we had learned to better manage his behaviours an opportunity presented itself to work for autism.west midlands as the Family Support Services Manager. It was when I was working with the families that I realized that their stories were so similar to mine, and that they like me felt isolated.

In 2004, having established that one of the best ways of offering parents support was to empower them by giving them the knowledge, training and skills required to managing crisis situations I became aware of the Managing Challenging Behaviour course which was an integral part of staff training at autism.west midlands. The course combined low arousal approaches to defusing incidents of physically challenging behaviour with practical skills to enable staff to withdraw safely and without causing pain to the individual in crisis. If all else failed staff were taught to safely restrain the individual. I was impressed by this approach as many of the low arousal strategies were ones which we as a family had used in one way or another with Christopher. What was different was the practical physical skills; if only someone had taught me these I would not have been as physically at risk as I had been in the past. Finally I was looking at something which formalized everything we wanted. I also knew that the parents I was now working with needed the very same help. I approached the training manager Sue Hatton, who was resistant at the time. She felt that training parents in physical interventions was problematic. Barriers were identified such as insurance, monitoring, getting the organization's approval. I did some research and could find no other organizations that were offering this type of training to parents. It seems that whilst it was often mandatory for staff in many organizations, parents were left to their own devices when the child was at home. However, I was so convinced that this training was the answer to many of the parents' problems that I became very persistent and eventually won the day. A one off pilot was agreed.

We decided to run the course over six evenings as experience had shown us that both main carers needed to attend together to ensure consistency of approach. At first we thought we should deliver it in the same way that it was delivered to staff…we soon learned that this could not be delivered to parents in the same way! The emotional impact on families was huge and relationship difficulties were not unusual. We built time in for families to talk about their experiences and we approached each part of the training in a family focused way. The pilot was a great success and needless to say that this was the first of many courses and we learned along the way what parents really needed and started to tell people through articles, conferences, workshops and word of mouth.

Studio III, the organization who devised the course, and in particular one of the founders/directors Dr Andy McDonnell, were very supportive of this work, which eventually led to him offering me the opportunity to join Studio III to develop family training nationally. Obviously I said YES and here I am and here is this book.

Andrea's voice

I have been a community nurse since 1986; back then the whole approach to challenging behaviour was completely different. The only information that I got was on the legal issues and was very much about what I couldn't do. I felt that this was unacceptable as my experience was that staff were floundering when it came to coping with physically challenging behaviour. I decided that something had to be done and so I adopted an ad hoc and longwinded approach to training. I was the only community nurse taking this approach and soon found parents asking for the same training. In 1998 I started my Master's in Learning Disabilities Studies. For my research I wanted to look at the whole issue of teaching parents. This was a thorny issue and I had been experiencing strong resistance from my community nurse colleagues, who felt that giving parents these skills would mean that parents would always resort to using these skills as the only way of dealing with challenging behaviour, leading to possible abuse and injury. They were also unhappy with the whole approach and didn't want to learn the skills themselves. I became very frustrated and isolated and eventually left my post to become a lecturer, which I suspect was a relief to them!

I still felt strongly that my research needed to be parent focused but I was advised that it would be easier to settle for a questionnaire asking staff their views. Luckily I was pointed in the direction of Dr Andy McDonnell, who championed my cause by smoothing the way within my local learning disability trust for a family to be identified for me to work with. Needless to say it was a family with many and complex difficulties. However, they were enthusiastic and very supportive of me and this research. Professionals were surprised at the positive difference the training made to this family and as a result I continue to work with the community nurses and families in this trust.

Being a senior lecturer affords me the opportunity to inspire the students that come my way to be sympathetic to the needs of parents and to be positive in their approach. I teach essential skills to all branches of nursing and whenever I can I will bring in issues that affect people with learning disabilities and their families. Since being at the university I have also developed training around holding children for medical procedures and hope eventually to have a national debate on this subject through the publication of my PhD thesis.

I have kept in touch with Studio III informally throughout the ensuing years and recently Andy came to see me telling me about this wonderful woman who was coming to Studio III to look at developing training for parents and he thought it would be great if we could write a book together. Obviously I said YES and so here I am and here is the book.

What will you get from reading this handbook?

This is a practical, honest, no nonsense handbook which we hope will give you the confidence, skills and knowledge to manage challenging behaviours in a positive way. It will help you take a look at how you and your family live together. There may be areas that you feel need to be changed; if so, this book will give you ideas and strategies to effect that change. The case studies, scenarios and anecdotes are not research based, but come from personal experience and the experiences shared with us on various training courses. By sharing these experiences both good and bad we hope that you will realize you are not alone and the problems you may be facing are being faced by many other families. All names have been changed to preserve confidentiality.

Autism is a complex and sometimes baffling condition and families are often left perplexed and dismayed by some of the behaviours their children display. With greater knowledge comes better understanding! We explore the common features of autism and the impact they have on the child and family. We will look at the causes of challenging behaviour and how our feelings and attitudes can dictate how we deal with those behaviours. Although we will explore tried and tested strategies for managing behaviours in general the focus of the book is how we manage in a crisis. The low arousal techniques we advocate will if practised consistently help families to navigate their way through what can be very difficult times.

One of the components of the six session practical course is the teaching of the use of physical interventions such as breaking away from grabs, hair pulling and biting and also as a last resort a safe way to restrain someone who is either in danger or endangering others. These skills cannot be learned from a textbook and therefore are not included. However, our experience has shown that if we can defuse situations before they become out of control, the need for physical interventions diminishes. It is this area that the book concentrates on.

'Family meltdown'

CHAPTER 1

Understanding Autism

Autism Spectrum Disorder (ASD) is an umbrella term used to describe a wide variety of conditions which all have common features. Your child may have been diagnosed with Autism Spectrum Disorder itself or one of the following terms:

- able autism

- Asperger Syndrome

- atypical autism

- autistic tendencies/traits/features

- classic autism

- high-functioning autism

- Kanner Syndrome

- Pervasive Developmental Disorder not otherwise specified (PDD NOS)

- Semantic Pragmatic Disorder (SPD).

As you can see this umbrella shelters a variety of named conditions. It can be very confusing for families, especially when they meet other families where their child has a different diagnosis to their own child, but whatever the diagnosis, we must remember that they will all have the same core difficulties. Some parents will say that they have been told that their child is 'mildly autistic'; this is not always helpful as it infers that it is only a 'small' problem which is not usually the case.

Autism Spectrum Disorder (ASD) refers to the wide differences there can be between individuals with regard to their intellectual functioning. Some children with autism will have severe learning disabilities, some will have moderate learning disabilities and some children will have average to above average intelligence. But even those with average intelligence can encounter severe problems in some areas of their lives.

> Johnny has a diagnosis of classic autism and severe learning disabilities. He has no spoken language and he prefers to sit in the corner of the sitting room where he will play with his favourite object, his father's snooker trophy. He will turn it upside down, lick the metal name plate and trace his finger along the lettering. He becomes extremely distressed if his 'toy' is removed.

> Peter has Asperger Syndrome, he has good verbal ability and attends a mainstream school. He usually manages well in class with support as long as he is able to have his favourite dinosaur figures on his desk. When another child took one of his figures Peter became very distressed and turned his desk and chair over and began kicking his support worker.

In one sense these children are at opposite ends of the spectrum. However, they experience similar distress when their 'toys' are removed.

Key facts about
Autism Spectrum Disorder (ASD)

- It is a life long complex developmental disorder which usually manifests itself within the second year of life.

- Boys are four times more likely to develop ASD than girls.

- Figures for the prevalence of ASD vary but National Autistic Society figures show it to be 1 in 110.

- It can co-exist with other disabilities such as Down Syndrome, epilepsy, cerebral palsy and Attention Deficit Hyperactivity Disorder (ADHD).

- The child may or may not have an intellectual disability.

- The consensus of opinion is that there is a genetic pre-disposition to developing ASD. Most research is concentrated in trying to identify the genes and triggers responsible.

- Most people with autism will also have problems with their sensory system.

- Autism is present in all national, cultural, racial and social groups.

- Certain parts of the autism brain develop and function differently from the non autism brain; this means that how they perceive, understand and interpret the world may be different. Understanding this is crucial if we are to make sense of their behaviour.

What are the common features of ASD?

All children diagnosed with ASD have been identified as having problems with functioning in three areas:

1. social interaction

2. social communication

3. social imagination.

This has become known as the *Triad of Impairment* and is still used on most diagnostic criteria today.

Human beings are generally social animals and our ability to make and maintain social relationships and communicate effectively is crucial for our emotional and mental wellbeing. If our understanding of ourselves and others is impaired then so too is our ability to function effectively in the social world.

Social interaction

Wing and Gould (1979) found that children with autism broadly fell into three categories, which may help you understand your child better.

Aloof – This child seems withdrawn and self-absorbed and seems to actively avoid contact with others and may become frightened and distressed when attempts are made to interact with them or include them in activities. They may only seek others out to meet their immediate needs. They are not moti-vated by pleasing people and so often do not co-operate with others.

'Aloof'

Passive – This child does not seek out nor actively engage with others but also does not resist when led into activities and contact with others. They may need constant encourage-ment to stay within the situation. They may play alongside other children but not join in with the game. They may have problems telling you what they like and dislike. Just because they do not resist does not mean that they are having a good time.

'Passive'

Active but odd – This child seems to want to interact with others and is happy to approach people but does not always do so appropriately, as they have little understanding of the unwritten social rules. They often relate better to adults than their peers. They may want to make friends but really lack the skills required. They may want to control all the games and may have trouble with turn taking. They may go too far when playing rough and tumble games. They may become upset when others break rules but can often break rules themselves. They may talk incessantly about something that interests them and not realize when others are bored, or not listening.

'Active but Odd'

Linda says:

I very soon learned with Christopher that any social interaction was always on his terms. When he wanted something
it was usually to meet his needs whether emotional or
physical. He seemed oblivious to my needs; he was unable
to respond appropriately to my emotions or understand
that I was tired or did not enjoy doing whatever it was
he wanted me to do. I spent endless hours either singing
the same repertoire of songs or telling the same stories or
watching the same videos all making his world safer and
more predictable but quite often driving me to the edge of

reason! It was also hard to accept that what I thought was a 'treat' or a 'good time' for Christopher was probably the opposite of that. I have a video taken of his fifth birthday which we held at a local disabilities sports club which had a fabulous soft play area and invited some non-autistic children as well as his new classmates at his MLD [moderate learning difficulties] school. Everyone seemed to have a good time but as I am filming I come across Christopher lying next to his dad in the ball pit with his thumb in his mouth and his eyes closed; his dad was softly singing his favourite lullaby into his ear.

Needless to say that was the last conventional birthday party we have thrown for him. Since then we have learned that for Christopher a picnic on a deserted wet and wind-swept beach eating sandwiches being dive bombed by a seagull is far more entertaining for him! We need to be aware that putting them in a situation that we think they should like in a vain attempt to get them to join in is a recipe for disaster – there are no winners and everyone ends up miserable.

However, we continued to set up what we considered safe social activities. We often host family get togethers but there is no pressure on Christopher to join in. His bedroom is his safe haven and gradually he began to come down to see what was going on! We ask people not to approach him but to respond when he approaches them. This seems to work and he will now often sit at the table with extended family usually for short bursts and seems to enjoy himself.

Jenny says:

My husband and I are both from really big families and it seems that every month there is some party or event to attend. We always felt under pressure to be there but when I see our son just sitting under the table while all his cousins are rushing about having a good time it breaks my heart. He will go off with one of his older cousins but they very soon get bored with him because he won't join in.

Michael says:

> My son Stephen has Asperger Syndrome. We are big rugby league supporters in our house and Stephen loves to collect and log the scores for all the league matches; he knew all the rules by the time he was eight years old. I managed to get him into our local club but after two weeks the coach rang me to say that the other boys were unhappy because Stephen was acting more like the referee!

It can be hard for families to accept that their child may not want parties or friends, or for those children that do to see them fail to make and maintain friendships. But we can do things to help our children develop these skills.

HELPING YOUR CHILD

- Virtually from birth we start to play with our children. We are very excited when our babies respond to us with their first smile. It is through play that typically developing children learn. For children with ASD interactive play does not come naturally and so we have to teach them to play. The first step is to make sure we are engaging the child at their level, as developmentally and emotionally they may be functioning at a much lower level than their chronological age. Just spending time with our children and playing alongside them initially without pressure is a good start. Our ultimate aim is to share activities with them so be aware of their attempts to interact and make sure you take advantage of them.

- If possible encourage older children to play with your child as they can be more accommodating by being more patient and less competitive. They can help teach turn taking, about losing, about listening to others and sharing.

- Understand that your child may feel threatened by the close proximity of others, and make sure that there is always a safe space for them to withdraw to. Accept that your child is not lonely in the conventional sense and understand that it is important to allow for their solitariness. We need to build trust gradually.

- Go at your child's pace when trying to develop interaction. Remember it is a developmental disorder and they may be emotionally much younger than their chronological age even if they have not been identified as having a learning difficulty. Children with ASD need to be taught to play as it is not something that comes naturally. Set up opportunities for social interaction in a non-threatening way.

- Try and identify what they like and dislike socially and use this knowledge when planning activities. Avoiding crowds is usually a good idea when organizing days out and holidays.

- Accept that social occasions may be too much for them and be realistic about what they can cope with. If they have a bad experience they are less likely to tolerate the next occasion. It is much better to spend a short time in a social setting and then withdrawing rather than staying too long and your child becoming agitated. Be prepared to change your plans if on the morning of the event your child is not going to be able to manage it. Remember often discretion is the better part of valour!

- Carol Gray's Social Stories™ (1994) can help your child understand how to behave in social situations, cope with change and give them strategies for coping. As long as your child has an understanding of the language they do not need to be able to read. The stories can be repeated by adults or taped and played back to the child until they are confident. For more information on Social StoriesTM please see our further reading list.

Social communication

Imagine you have just arrived alone in a different country. You have no knowledge of the people, the language or the social rules. How anxious are you likely to be? Have you ever tried to communicate with someone who speaks a different language to you? Either you fall into an uncomfortable silence or you resort to gesticulation and pictures. Olga Bogdashina (2005) says that maybe children with autism 'speak' a different language.

> Verbal language is a sort of foreign language for them. And as they do not learn it naturally earlier in their lives, we have to help them master their second language with the support of their 'first language' if we want to share a means of communication with them. (p.32)

Having a shared language is a key component to helping us bond in our social groups. We use it to express and share our emotions, debate and argue and express our opinions, share interests and passions and impart information. Most of us are born with an innate desire to communicate for social purposes. Individuals with autism often do not develop their language beyond using it for the purpose of getting their emotional and physical needs met. It seems they do not understand the real purpose of communication. They will all have difficulty with both the use of and the understanding of language.

We can use the spectrum analogy again to look at the differences in language acquisition for individuals with autism. Some may never develop speech, some may have a few words and phrases and use a lot of echolaic (repetitive) speech while others will have apparently excellent verbal skills but may have problems with intonation and volume. But just because an individual has good verbal skills it does not necessarily mean they have good understanding. Conversely an individual with no speech may in fact have a good understanding of what is being said to them.

> Kevin is 18 years old and has very good verbal skills. He can recite several of the plays of William Shakespeare; he particularly likes to recite Julius Caesar and he is word perfect. But when he is asked what the play is actually about he cannot really say.

We must remember this is a communication disorder, not a language disorder. Fifty per cent of language is non-verbal. Our posture, gestures, facial expressions, the tone and intonation of our voice all give us clues to the meaning of what is being said. For a child with autism deciphering these messages will be difficult.

Some children have a literal understanding of language and can become very confused when we use euphemisms, metaphors, colloquialisms and slang. We tend to use verbal shorthand particularly with people we are familiar with. The confusion for someone with autism is immense. For example in the following conversations that people have with Billy:

Mum: 'Put the kettle on.'
    Billy thinks 'Put it on what or where?'

Teacher: 'Pull your socks up.'
    Billy looks down at his socks and is confused when he sees they are not down.

Teacher: 'Billy, can you open the window?'

Billy: 'Yes.' (Billy doesn't move.)

Teacher: 'Billy, will you open the window now please?' (Billy gets up and opens the window.)

You want to take Billy to the park.
    'Come on, Billy, get your shoes and coat on and we can go to the park and play on the swings and we can have an ice cream.' Billy due to his processing delay does not respond so you say 'Come on, Billy, if we don't go now we won't have time before we have to go to grandma's. You find your shoes and I'll get your coat.' Now Billy has to process this new information – it is estimated that there is an average 9–10 second delay in their processing skills (although this can vary widely). You are now frustrated and losing patience and Billy is anxious and confused.

Try reducing the words…

    'Billy, coat, shoes, park.'

Using his name to get his attention is essential. Don't assume that just because there are only you two in the room he will think you are talking to him – remember your child does not understand the social use of communication. Pictures, objects of reference (holding the coat aloft), exaggerated gestures; all help him to get a picture of what is expected of him.

HELPING YOUR CHILD

- Simplify your language. It does not come naturally for us to do this and many parents worry that by restricting their use of language in this way their children will not learn. But there are plenty of opportunities to use language with your child by perhaps giving a running commentary on what you or they are doing or by commenting on the activity of others whilst out or when reading books or watching videos.

- Always use their name first to get their attention. Give one instruction at a time in the sequence you want things to happen. Giving too much information can be very confusing for your child. You are more likely to get a result and reduce his frustration if he can respond to your requests in stages.

- Keep facial expressions and gestures simple and clear. Focus on your child and the task in hand.

- Use additional visual clues to help them understand (pictures, real objects, gestures); digital cameras are essential equipment! Take pictures of activities and places you visit regularly and significant people in their lives.

- Be sensitive to your child's attempts to communicate; always try to respond and encourage them. Sometimes we can be distracted when we are busy or stressed. By not responding to their attempts we are missing vital opportunities to build our relationship with them and extend their communication skills.

- Set up situations which will encourage the child to attempt to communicate. Don't always anticipate his needs and requests; encourage him to 'ask' for his favourite toy or a drink or video.

- Give the person time to respond – remember they may have a processing delay. If you do need to repeat an instruction or request, think about what you said. Was it clear and unambiguous? If so repeat again slowly; if it wasn't then rephrase and give more time for your child to respond.

- Use concrete language whenever possible. Later, soon, shortly, maybe, in a while are all abstract concepts. Avoid euphemisms and colloquialisms. Your child may well have difficulty understanding irony and sarcasm and may become very upset if teased. Remember good verbal ability can mask poor understanding.

Social imagination

Confusion can arise when we talk about imagination. Does this mean your child cannot be creative? Certainly not: as you are probably aware there are many examples of people with autism as poets, writers of fiction and artists. What it does mean is that they may have a problem with thinking flexibly and imagining the future.

Try to think how we operate on a day to day basis. We wake up in the morning and think about the day ahead which may or may not have a plan. There may be lots of uncertainty as some plans haven't been confirmed. We may even be hoping for a surprise call from a friend to whisk us off to lunch! We may phone the doctor to see if they could fit us in at some point and be willing to change our plans to accommodate this. The 'to do list' carried over from yesterday may have more ticks on it by the end of the day! While driving to an appointment we see road works and think of another way around to cut out time. In other words we have a plan B; we are able to be flexible in our thinking; we can imagine another scenario and shift our thinking. Yes, we may get stressed when things don't go according to plan but on the other hand we may be completely exhilarated by new experiences or a surprise visit.

An individual with ASD often cannot think of plan B because their problem with social imagination means they have difficulty anticipating what is going to happen in the future. They often live in the here and now and have great difficulty shifting their thinking to accommodate another plan.

The world and the people in it seem chaotic and unpredictable and they need structure and routine and sameness to give them predictability. Any change may provoke huge anxiety.

Jackie says:

It seems that our whole life is ruled by David's need for sameness and routine. We all have to sit in the same seats for meals, and we have to sit down for dinner at exactly six o'clock. He becomes very agitated when someone is late. If we have to change his route on the way to school he screams and tries to get out of the car.

Given the unpredictability of our world it is not surprising that people with autism adopt ritualized behaviours and routines to make an unsafe and confusing world safe and predictable.

A mainstream school was having a problem with the behaviour of a seven-year-old boy with autism. On further investigation it seems that the real problem was at playtime, when he was kicking the children. When we spoke to the staff it seems that David would go out to play and the staff would tell him to 'join in with the others'. Already we can see that for someone with autism this is very difficult – he doesn't understand the rules of social interaction, he doesn't know how to approach the children in a positive way and he is unsure of what is expected of him. On the first day he approaches the group of children as directed but because of his communication difficulty and his lack of social understanding he becomes very anxious and kicks one of the children. The staff member goes over and tells him off and makes him stand by her for the rest of break. At last he knows what he is supposed to be doing! Next day he goes out to play and is told to go and join in the game. Again he is anxious and so again kicks the same child and again the staff member goes to fetch him, tells him off, makes him stand by her for the whole of break. Again he is relieved. Can you see what is happening? This has now become a very predictable routine; he has learned what to do to get predictability!

Once the staff understood what was happening they instigated an activity for him during break times, led by some of the older children. Remember your child will have difficulty with self-direction. Free time without some sort of structure can be very difficult for them to cope with. They may fall back on negative behaviours familiar to them in an attempt to give order to the chaos.

This inflexibility also leads to problems with generalizing. Your child may learn a skill in one situation but find it difficult to use those skills in another situation. You may feel a great sense of accomplishment the day your child finally ties his shoe laces before school but find he can't perform the same task when at school.

Transitions are particularly difficult for individuals with ASD. These can be major transitions such as changing school or small transitions such as moving from one task to another. We need to prepare them for change and major transitions need to be planned giving adequate time for a gradual introduction. Your child may adopt behaviours and devices to help them cope with these changes. As long as they are not dangerous do not try to stop them as they will help reduce your child's anxiety until they are used to the change.

Linda says:

> I remember the agitation I used to feel as the school bus drew up and waited for Christopher to appear. Of course he would then start his routine of rewinding his video tape, turning all the lights off, straightening the cushions, while the driver was playing the steering wheel bongo. Because of my increasing anxiety I would chivvy Christopher up and try and stop his routine until I realized just how important it all was to him, how unless he was able to complete these routines he would be a very agitated and stressed young man on arrival at school. I developed another layer to my already thickening skin and relaxed into the moment waiting patiently until all routines were completed and smiled sweetly at the driver as I put him on the bus!

Theory of mind

This concrete thinking also affects their 'theory of mind', that is your child's ability to see that other people have different thoughts, needs and ideas from themselves. Again this can make them appear to be selfish and egocentric. This is not by choice; they genuinely have real difficulty in seeing the world from another person's perspective.

Understanding what others are feeling and thinking is an essential skill for positive social interaction and deciphering the 'hidden' meaning in communication. This lack of understanding can lead to poor empathy, so the child may not respond as we would to another's emotional state. They may not be able to predict the consequences of their own actions.

A parent recounted the story of when she suffered a heart attack at home. She was very proud of the fact that her 16-year-old autistic son knew to dial 999 and alert the neighbour. However, as the ambulance door was closing the last words she heard were her son shouting 'Who's going to cook my dinner?' Selfish? No, autistic!

When we talk about someone winding us up and doing things on purpose for attention, etc., we need to think about theory of mind. Knowing how to wind someone up takes a good understanding of that person. Their behaviour may have the effect of winding us up but whether that was the child's intention is in doubt. It is more likely that they were seeking a predictable response.

Central coherence theory

Individuals with autism are thought to have weak central coherence, which means that their ability to gather information and put it all together to give it a higher meaning is impaired; in other words they are more likely to focus on the detail and not see the bigger picture. They may be oblivious to what is going on around them as they concentrate their efforts in one small area of concern. This can mean they have a problem seeing things in context. It is as if they can see all the individual pieces of the jigsaw but not the finished picture.

> Johnny was crossing the road when the pedestrian light changed to red. He stopped in the middle of the road which caused car drivers to shout at him to get out of the way; he became very agitated and did not know what to do.

HELPING YOUR CHILD

- Most children with ASD respond better to visual cues, so offer visual support to help them predict what is going to happen next. Having a pictorial schedule of their day ready as soon as they wake will help reduce anxiety. Getting the family off to work and school will be far less stressful for all concerned.

- Be consistent. In a world that they find chaotic your child will be looking for stability and sameness. They will have problems working out what is expected of them if boundaries and rules change all the time.

monday to friday			
7.30 am	Wake up call	shower	brush teeth
8.00 am	Breakfast	Medication	
8.30 am	Bus for school		
3.25 pm	Return from school		
5.00 pm	Evening meal		
5.30 pm	Free time		
8.30 pm	Shower	Supper	
9.00 pm	Medication	Bedtime	

'Sequence plan for the day'

- Make sure that you and the family act as predictably as possible. How we react and respond can depend on our mood and feelings at the time. Again your child will be confused if they cannot predict your reactions.

- Have clear and predictable routines. After the structure and routine of school it is tempting to just muddle through the evenings, weekends and school holidays, but for your child these times can be particularly difficult and many parents find them very stressful. By planning ahead and sticking to a routine, stress levels can be reduced for all the family.

- Introduce changes gradually; because of their problems with thinking flexibly you need to prepare your child for any changes. Again using pictures can make future events real.

- If your child has an obsession, do not try to stop it. In time, you may be able to limit it; in the meantime use it positively. It can be used as an aid to learning and help with transitions. It can also be used to motivate them to complete tasks: 'first this', 'then this' works well.

- Making choices can be difficult; offering two options may be all that some children can cope with. Open ended questions such as 'What would you like for breakfast?' should be avoided; better to say 'would you like Weetabix or Corn Flakes?' If this causes confusion show the boxes as visual clues.

first this

then this

'First this, then this'

- Your child will have difficulty recognizing their own emotions. Recognition of emotions such as anger and fear is the first step to managing them. Use pictures and exaggerated gestures to indicate sad, happy, angry, scared. Comment when you see him and others displaying these emotions. Describe the physical feelings such as tight throat, tummy hurting, etc. We will look at strategies for managing anger in future chapters.

'Sensory overload'

Sensory issues

How we perceive and experience the world is dictated by the information we gather through our sensory system. Sight, sounds, smells, taste and touch all work together to give us experiences. If our sensory system is not working properly then our perception of the world may become distorted. Besides the five senses we all know about we have two other 'hidden' senses:

1. *Vestibular* (our sense of balance)

    The fact that our feet are firmly on the ground is due to the earth's gravitational pull but it is our sense of balance that keeps us upright. It is located in our inner ear and it tells our brain where our body is in space and what speed and direction we are going.

2. *Proprioception* (body awareness)

    This sense is situated in our muscles and joints; it tells our brain where our body is in relation to our environment. It also tells us where our individual body parts are and how they are moving. If we put our arm out behind us even though we can't see it we will know where it is. Another example is that it tells our hand and fingers how much pressure to exert when picking up an object. We would use more pressure to pick up a glass than to pick up a plastic cup.

The importance of the sensory problems that individuals with autism face has only relatively recently been fully acknowledged. Some have written extensively on their sensory experiences and perceptual difficulties and these accounts and careful observation have helped us to understand the problems that children with little or no communication could also be experiencing. Many extreme negative behaviours can be caused by sensory problems.

> The corridors and halls of almost any mainstream school are a constant tumult of noises echoing, fluorescent lights (a particular source of visual and auditory stress for people on the autistic spectrum), bells ringing, people bumping into each other, the smells of cleaning products and so on. For anyone with the sensory hyper-sensitivities and processing problems typical of an autistic spectrum condition, the result is that we often spend most of the day perilously close to sensory overload. (Sainsbury 2000)

Sensory integration is the ability to take in information through our senses which is then processed by the brain. The information is then analysed and a response is actioned. This response may be a thought, feeling or behaviour. The process is as follows:

- *Registration*: We become aware of the sensation.

- *Orientation*: We pay attention to it.

- *Interpretation*: We use current information and refer to past experiences for comparison.

- *Organization*: This occurs when our brain decided what to do in response to the sensation.

- *Execution*: What we actually do in response to the sensation.

When the system is not working properly it can lead to either:

Hypersensitivity: the sensory channel is too open; as a result too much stimulation is allowed in to the brain and it becomes overloaded. If we use a sieve analogy it is as if when straining a sauce the holes are so big all the unwanted bits go straight into the pan.

Or

Hyposensitivity: the channel is not open enough; as a result too little of the stimulation gets in and the brain is deprived of information. This time the sieve holes are too close together and the sauce only drips through and most stays in the sieve.

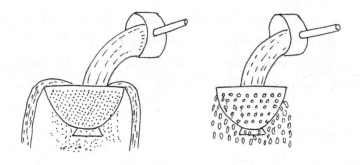

Sieves

Individuals can be hypersensitive in one area and hyposensitive in another. Their sensitivity may change on a daily basis. Some individuals may only be able to process information through one sensory channel at a time.

> Peter was looking down at the floor whilst his teacher was giving him a verbal instruction. She thought he wasn't paying attention and told him to look at her whilst she was speaking. Peter was unable to complete the task and his teacher chastised him. Peter became very agitated and ran out of the classroom.

Peter was not able to process information through his auditory and visual channel at the same time. Because he had to look at the teacher he was unable to process the verbal instruction.

What for us is normal sensory experiences can be frightening and confusing for the individual with autism; it may even be painful. Many extreme behaviours can be reactions to distorted sensory experiences.

Problems and strategies

Sense	Hyper	Hypo	What may help hyper	What may help hypo
Sight (visual). Activated by light.	May have distorted vision. May find bright lights painful. May be easily distracted by tiny objects, busy wallpaper and wall decorations. Problems with eye contact.	May use peripheral vision as central vision blurred. Problems with depth perception. Unable to judge distances. May bang into things.	Use diffused, soft lighting. Remove fluorescent lighting if possible. Use dimmer switches. Use blinds or blackout curtains in bedrooms. Offer sunglasses.	Keep floor areas clear. Mark edge of stairs and steps.
Hearing (auditory) system. Most common sensory problem for individuals with ASD.	Noises seem louder, sounds can be distorted, unable to filter out background noises. May have difficulty concentrating.	May only hear in one ear. May enjoy making their own noise. May enjoy particularly noisy places/ activities.	Ear plugs, iPod with familiar favourite music. Reduce noise with double glazing insulation and soft flooring. Keep volume down on TV/ music system. Do not have more than one on at a time. Prepare them before entering noisy environment.	Try introducing sounds at differing pitches and volumes. Use sing-a-long activities to help them engage with you.

(continued)

Sense	Hyper	Hypo	What may help hyper	What may help hypo
Touch (tactile) sense. Receptors on skin's surface. Detects pain, temperature, pressure.	Light touch can be painful. Clothes can feel uncomfortable, especially new clothes. Having hair brushed and washed can be difficult.	High pain threshold. May squeeze or hold other too tightly. May self-injure. May squeeze into tight spaces or like heavy weights on them.	Teach them to brush hair/teeth themselves. Tell them when you are going to touch them. Wash new clothes several times before wearing, cut out 'scratchy' labels.	Weighted blankets will help them sleep or sleeping bags. Weighted jackets. Body warmer snug fit. Neoprene suits. Massage.
Taste (gustatory) system. Receptors on the tongue indicate sweet, sour, bitter, salty, hot and cold.	May only eat bland foods, have problems with texture. May not eat crunchy or lumpy foods.	May eat non-edibles such as soil, cigarette ends, flowers (pica). May like very strong tastes.	Introduce different textures and tastes slowly, do not make an issue at meal time, try and relax.	Offer strong tasting foods, keep chemical cleaners, etc., out of reach.
Smell (olfactory) system.	Finds certain smells overpowering. May become distressed at changes in perfumes, washing powders, etc. May have toileting problems.	May have no sense of smell. May not notice strong odours. May be attracted to strong odours leading to problems with smearing, etc. May lick objects.	Only use fragrance-free household and personal hygiene products wherever possible.	Have a stock of strong smelling products to act as motivators.
Balance (vestibular) system. Crucial for maintaining our balance and posture.	May have problems with physical activities, sports. May have problems stopping, starting and changing direction.	Will compensate by rocking, spinning, swinging.	Use visual clues for start, stop, etc.	Use outdoor activities such as swing, roundabout, seesaws, trampoline.
Body awareness (proprioception) system. Positioned in deep muscles and joints.	Problems with writing, tying shoe laces, doing up buttons, etc.	May invade others' space. May bump into people and objects. May lean against others.	Any activity to help with fine motor skills. Threading, lacing etc.	Position furniture around edge of room. Keep floors clear. Teach body awareness and appropriate space, etc.

Each child may have a different experience. One child may love the loud sound of the washing machine or vacuum cleaner, whilst another may press their hands over their ears and dive under the table. They may have multiple sensory problems which means they react to sensory stimuli in a very negative way.

Linda says:

> Christopher has many sensory problems. He will try and correct his problems by bouncing and squeezing himself into small spaces. He will often hit himself hard on his body and head and curl his toes up and flex his tummy muscles. Last year he had a nasty accident as he bounced so hard on the toilet that it broke and cut him very badly. He also rocks backwards and forward and he has broken the suspension on two of our cars. He seems very clumsy and will often walk into door jambs and furniture.
>
> We have worked out activities such as walking, swimming, trampoline and massage which go some way to helping him.

Emotional overload

For many individuals with ASD just the interaction and demands placed by others is too much for them to come to terms with emotionally. Eye contact is especially difficult and there are many personal accounts of how eye contact can actually be painful. Individuals may react badly to any sign of emotional warmth or praise. For parents this can be especially difficult. But we need to be aware that we may have to temper our feelings and not overwhelm our children.

Linda says:

Christopher would quite often want to be with us but seemed to be unable to cope with us in the same room. Many times he would go into the conservatory with doors shut and we would spend hours singing songs and repeating his favourite phrases. It was as if he needed the barrier of the glass doors to be able to cope with the interaction.

By understanding the way the sensory problems affect our child we will be able to adjust the environment to make sure it is as sensory friendly as possible and try to avoid sensory overload.

Just as an example, think about the experience of going to the local shopping centre. First, it is usually full of people, all talking at once, going in different directions, the lighting is bright, the smell changes as you go past the perfume shop, the traditional sweet shop, the candle shop, there may be musak playing, there are escalators, all in all a massive sensory experience. Many parents report that shopping with their child usually ends in tears.

We know of several families who shop at the local 24-hour supermarket at two in the morning to avoid the crowds. What else do you do when your child never sleeps?

Working out where each child's problems lie is not an easy task especially if they are unable to report their experiences. We rely on careful observation and assessment. Specialist occupational therapists, speech and language therapists are the professionals most likely to make these assessments.

Every child who is diagnosed with ASD should have access to a full sensory assessment, but sadly this is not always the case due to availability of therapists and resources. However, it is an essential piece in the jigsaw and until we know where their problems lie we cannot help them. Olga Bogdashina (2005) has compiled a sensory questionnaire at the back of her book for carers to use. Once we have a sensory profile we can use this information to make sure that the environment and activities and equipment we provide for them meet their individual need.

Movement difficulties in autism

Donnellan and Leary (1995) give another explanation for the problems faced by individuals with autism. They assert that they may be experiencing movement difficulties which may result in problems with starting and stopping combining movements, executing and switching movements. This may affect their speech and thoughts, perceptions, memories and emotions.

It may impair their learning about self; learning about textures, tastes, temperatures; learning about size; learning about orientation of body in space; development of perceptual skills and independence from others.

Examples of movement disturbance in autism

These behaviours may be familiar: repetitive movements, fixed expression, tics, grimacing, teeth grinding, abnormal gait, blocking/freezing, unusual postures, over-activity, rocking, problems with initiation/stopping, lack of inhibition, spinning, twirling, mutism, hand flapping, tiptoe walking, dyspraxia, poor co-ordination, abnormal startle response, problems with speech volume/rhythm, stuttering, slow speech, uncontrollable laughing.

Implications of movement disturbance in autism

All communication requires movement and so if an individual experiences movement difficulties then they will also have problems with communication.

Emotions, thoughts and memories may require small neurological movements and therefore problems in this area may mean that the individual will perceive the world differently. They may take longer to process information and will rely on their self-devised accommodations to help them overcome their problems.

Accommodations

Donnellan and Leary (1995) use the term *accommodation* when they are referring to strategies devised by the individual with ASD that directly help them adjust or work through his or her problem. These strategies may include touch, gestures, rhythm, music, specific carers. They will be different for each person. Sadly if the individual's accommodation is a member of staff, then difficulties arise when that person leaves or moves to work with another.

> Every morning John stands at the top of the stairs singing his four favourite songs. When he has finished a member of staff has to stand at the bottom and count each step as John stands on them. He cannot move until this is done.
>
> James cannot go through the doorways at home until he has kissed the frame three times.

We probably all use accommodations. Sportsmen/women are notorious for their 'idiosyncrasies'. The great English rugby player Jonny Wilkinson could not kick the ball unless he had first completed an elaborate hand movement. Tennis players can be seen bouncing the ball several times or blowing on the ball. How many times do you check that you have locked your front door before you can leave for an important event?

We may be mistaken in thinking that these coping mechanisms are self-stimulating or obsessional behaviours. If Donnellan and Leary are right then we need to be mindful of the implications. If we try and curb or stop or interrupt these behaviours, the individual may react badly or have great difficulty in moving onto the next task/situation.

We can now see just how complex ASD is. Our knowledge has increased significantly over the past 20 years but we are still only scratching the surface. What is abundantly clear, however, is that the experience of children with ASD is at times frightening, bewildering and confusing; is it any wonder therefore that they often react with behaviours that we find challenging?

Chapter 2

Understanding Challenging or Distressed Behaviour

Billy fuming

It is not surprising, then, that as a reaction to our unpredictable and confusing world many people with autism display challenging behaviours we find difficult to cope with, but first let's look at what we mean by challenging behaviour. It's a term used by professionals to describe behaviours displayed by individuals who already have a diagnosed condition. We can all be challenging to others at times but we do not get labelled in this way. The most often quoted definition comes from Emerson (1995); he defined it as:

> A culturally abnormal behaviour of such intensity, frequency or duration that the physical safety of the person or others is likely to be placed in serious jeopardy, or behaviour that is likely to seriously limit the use of, or result in the person being denied access to ordinary community facilities.

This definition is useful because it does not just look at physically challenging behaviours but also those behaviours that could be seen as socially unacceptable or stressful for others.

> Arfan has difficulty coping with bright lights and also reacts very strongly when he hears a baby crying. He has kicked and bitten his parents when in a situation he finds difficult. His parents are worried about taking him into public places in case they see a family with a baby.

> Jack has pica (he picks up anything on the floor and puts it in his mouth). He also makes loud noises when he is excited and will run up to people and look in their pockets for handkerchiefs. His family find it really difficult to go out in a public place with Jack as they get very embarrassed when he approaches strangers and when people turn to look when he makes a noise.

Both of these situations fit in with Emerson's definition as the behaviours are discouraging parents from giving their children access to *ordinary community facilities*. In Arfan's case there is also the problem of his physically aggressive behaviours which may be putting his or others' physical safety at risk.

Intensity, frequency and duration are also identified by Emerson as key factors in considering behaviours as challenging.

Our personal experience of the behaviour, how we feel about that behaviour and how others react to it may make it seem more intense to us than it perhaps does to others not so closely involved. Also if the behaviour has become more frequent we may feel its intensity further. If the behaviours we have identified as challenging are occurring frequently then we are more likely to feel worn down by them and if we have been exposed to a behaviour for a long period of time we may feel that we are coming to the end of our tether.

> Balvinder has a severe learning disability and no spoken language. Over the last two years he has become more physically challenging and often bites his mother. She coped in the early days as his outbursts were not frequent (probably monthly). However, since he started at a new school he has outbursts on an almost daily basis. His mother now feels she cannot cope any longer and is requesting a residential placement for Balvinder.

The language we use to describe these behaviours will influence the way others view our children. Many parents have reported that trying to access community activities can be difficult if your child is labelled as challenging. Phoebe Caldwell (Caldwell and Horwood 2008) prefers to use the term *distressed behaviour* rather than challenging behaviour. We have to say, we're with Phoebe on this one! When someone reacts negatively to others, their environment or sensory overload, it is usually because they are in distress; from now on that's the term we will use – as it is distressing for the young person and distressing for the family.

Tolerances

The following exercise is a good starting point to check out how you feel about certain behaviours that your child may display. As a family, give each of the behaviours listed below a score: 5 being the highest given for a behaviour you find very difficult to tolerate and 1 being the lowest for any behaviour you don't have any trouble coping with. What we expect you to find is that your scores will not be the same.

> Linda finds spitting is a five as is biting and also finds vomit hard to deal with but copes very well with poo! Her husband on the other hand really cannot cope with the repetitive questioning where she seems to be able to screen it out. He is also much better with vomit than she is. Andrea struggles with people throwing large objects! But she copes well with anything to do with bodily fluids (that's the nurse coming out!).

This exercise is really useful as it helps you to understand how each of you feel about certain behaviours and can help toward the goal of working as a family team.

Acknowledging our tolerance level is important, as how we cope with a behaviour will determine how we deal with it! We don't live in a vacuum and lots of stresses and pressures are brought to bear on our lives. The following are known to affect our tolerance levels.

Behaviour tolerances exercise

Behaviour	1	2	3	4	5
Kicking					
Punching					
Slapping					
Biting					
Pinching					
Hair pulling					
Verbal abuse					
Smearing					
Spitting					
Inappropriate masturbation					
Vomiting and regurgitation					
Damage to property					
Running off					
Constant questioning					
Repetitive phrases					
Obsessions					
Ritualistic behaviours					
Screaming					
Non-compliance/withdrawal					
Please feel free here to add any others you experience					

Tiredness – The more tired we are, the less tolerant we become. Your child may not understand that you are tired and that after two hours of continual repetitive questioning you have reached breaking point. You need to acknowledge just how much you can cope with and when you need to take a break or ask for assistance.

Environment – Where the behaviour occurs is important as we often have the embarrassment factor. Either we do not tolerate behaviours that embarrass us in public but put up with them at home or conversely we may stick to our guns at home but cave in when in public to avoid a scene. This sends mixed messages to our children and also confuses them!

Significant others – How others react to our children and our way of dealing with them will also affect how we tolerate the behaviour. Quite often our self-esteem is really low and if someone tells us we are wrong in managing a situation we may go against our instincts and react badly to a behaviour our child is displaying. One parent who attended the course said the best thing he got out of it was that he felt strong enough to tell his own father, who thought his management style was 'too soft', to mind his own business!

Our values and beliefs – We know one father who rated the destruction of property as a five and he said he had intervened to stop his son breaking things and the situation had deteriorated to the point that both he and his son had been hurt. When we looked at why this was such a problem for him, he told us that as a child money was in very short supply and his father would insist that each toy that was played with was then returned to its box until the next time it was to be played with. Once he realized why he felt like he did he was able to quell the rising feelings of anger each time something got broken and walked away rather than confront his son; unsurprisingly the destructive behaviour lessened. It may be when reading this you can think of situations where your own values or beliefs, whether they be religious, cultural or family, have impacted negatively on the way you have coped with your child's behaviour.

Our relationship with our child – Sadly when we have experienced some behaviours, especially if they are physically aggressive, our relationship with our child is bound to be affected and we may feel angry and resentful, hurt and scared. Being able to step back and detach ourselves is really important and may help.

Our previous experience – This may work in two ways. We may become 'immune' to some behaviours as we get used to them and so we become more tolerant; conversely, overexposure to them may just push us to our limits and beyond.

Stress – It goes without saying that our stress levels will be higher than most, not only for the very fact of caring for someone with complex needs, but we may be experiencing other problems such as stressful jobs, relationship problems, financial worries. As our stress levels rise so our tolerance levels go down. The last chapter of this book explores the effects of stress and gives you tips on how to reduce stress in your life.

Physical health – The problem with being a parent is that you can't phone in sick! If we are feeling unwell we may not be able to physically cope with behaviours we normally manage. We discuss your health further in the last chapter of this book.

Understanding the causes! – The more we understand about the autism the more tolerant we become. If we stop thinking that they are doing things on purpose, being manipulative, seeking attention, being disruptive, naughty, cheeky, rude then we come to see the behaviours in a different light. It allows us to look at the individual rather than focus on the behaviour. In Chapter 4 ('Using video') we have included an exercise for you to complete which looks at your thoughts about challenging behaviour which complements this section on tolerances.

So what are the causes of distressed behaviour?

There is no one cause of distressed behaviour and the complexity of autism means that it not always easy to establish a cause every time; however, there are many things that do have an effect on behaviours. The good news is most of the causes can be prevented once we have a handle on the autism!

Physical health – Whenever behaviour takes a turn for the worse, the first thing we need to check out is their *physical health*. We know for instance that people with autism do not always register pain in the same way nor do they always express it as we would. There are many examples of people having a tooth abscess or appendicitis and even broken limbs but not showing outward signs except for deterioration in their behaviour. Research is telling us that more and more children and adults are being diagnosed with diabetes. If your child's blood sugar levels are too low (hypoglycaemia) or too high (hyperglycaemia) this can have an impact upon their behaviour and cause a deterioration. Urinary tract infections can cause confusion. Both of these illnesses can be detected through testing your child's urine.

Pain is a subjective emotional response and physical experience which we feel as real in ourselves but can only interpret in our children through their pain behaviours. Remember that pain is usually an unpleasant experience and can cause your child to feel stressed. If your child has visited hospital recently the nurses may have shown them pictures of happy and sad faces as a way of helping your child evaluate how much pain they are feeling. Although not perfect (as your child may not be able to distinguish from other sources of distress) happy/sad faces may help.

Lack of structure and predictability – We can't stress just how important this is to someone with autism; we all need structure and routine. We are both Virgos and, comparing notes, can't count the amount of time we have had a day off and not actually achieved anything because we didn't have a plan! Many families report that weekends and school holidays are very difficult; not surprisingly we tend to be more relaxed about routine at these times but as we have said before 'free time' can be a nightmare for someone with autism. Having structure and predictability in the family home is not always easy! But having a plan for the day so everyone knows what they are doing really does have a beneficial effect for everyone. For your child with ASD the plan needs to be visual such as a photo sequence to explain what is happening on that day.

Anxiety – Given the unpredictable and frightening world in which people with autism find themselves it is not surprising that they suffer very high levels of anxiety. This will often spill over into violent outbursts where they will either hurt themselves or others. If we can reduce the anxiety we will also reduce the incidents of distressed behaviours. By understanding the sensory issues faced by your child and the need for structure and predictability anxiety levels can be greatly reduced.

Sensory overload – We all perceive and experience the world through our senses. When we say 'making sense of the world' we mean just that: take away all our senses and we do not function. If our senses are out of kilter then our perception of the world is different; if we are unable to filter out different stimuli then life becomes unbearable. Behaviours are often adopted to allow us to escape from situations we find intolerable.

Frustration – Communication problems between us and the person with autism often lead to frustration on both sides. Also not being able to complete tasks set by others may lead to frustration. Sometimes our expectations do not take into account the fluctuating abilities of our children.

Demands and requests – Finally one of the main causes of distressed behaviour is carers. Research carried out by Studio III showed that 65 per cent of incidents of distressed behaviour were preceded by a demand or a request from a carer. The good news is that if we reduce our demands and requests in times of crisis, then we will also be able to reduce the incidents of distressed behaviour. We will examine this more closely when we look at low arousal (see Chapter 3).

Schopler and Mesibov (1994) use the 'tip of the iceberg' approach, in that what we see above sea level is the aggression, self-injury or ritualistic behaviours, but it is what is below sea level that we need to tackle – the causes of the visible behaviours (such as communication difficulties, lack of intuitive understanding, inability to predict or control their environment, sensory issues, etc.). By dealing with the causes rather than the behaviours themselves we will be far better able to effect change.

The iceberg analogy

One of the couples on a parent course we ran came one week at the end of their tether. Their eight-year-old son was throwing toilet rolls out of the bathroom window and they were landing on the next door neighbour's prize fruit bushes. Understandably the neighbour had complained and was threatening to go to the landlord if it kept happening. We asked the rest of the parents what they thought. 'Lock the window' (tried this – he smashed it). 'Hide the toilet rolls' (tried this – he became so distressed he bit his mother).

To help this family we used the iceberg analogy. Why does he need to be throwing toilet rolls out of the window? What is he getting from this? What is below the surface? We asked what exactly did he do? His family said he would take the toilet roll, unravel a fair length and then throw it out and watch it drift down. We knew he often played with things close to his eyes and so asked could this be a sensory issue, could he be enjoying the visual stimulation? What else could he use rather than toilet rolls? How about ribbon? Next meeting the parents came in looking very pleased with themselves. They had bought several lengths of brightly coloured ribbon and tied each length to the window riser and had helped him throw them out and then retrieve them – they were amazed as he squealed with delight and stood for several hours throwing them out and pulling them back in. Everyone was happy, including the neighbour! The solution was only found when we asked the right question: *why* was he doing it? It wasn't the toilet rolls that were important; that was just a tool he had found.

Most behaviours have a function; by this we mean they have a reason, such as:

- *communication and interaction* – to get someone to take notice of them

- *sensation* – it may meet a sensory or emotional need

- *tangible benefit* – to get something they want, food, drink, toy

- *demand avoidance* – refusal to co-operate

- *social avoidance* – to avoid social situations they do not feel able to participate in.

As parents we need to be able to work out what causes the behaviours if we are to manage them properly. This takes careful observation. Using a diary may help you pinpoint when, where and with whom behaviours occur. A widely used system is the *ABC of behaviour*.

ABC stands for Antecedent, Behaviour and Consequence.

Antecedent – This could be the setting (such as an environment where there is too much going on, or a setting where there is nothing of interest to your child's attention, or a setting where they are not getting any attention from anybody, or there is something in the environment which is irritating them or somebody they dislike is present); an internal state (such as your child is in pain, or medication has affected their mood, hormones); or a specific event (such as being expected to join in the party games...the behaviour may then function as a means of escape; being required to do something they don't want to do...again the behaviour may be used as a means of escape, having something taken away) which may have an influence on whether or not a particular behaviour happens immediately or shortly afterwards. Information should record the behaviour(s) immediately prior to the distressed behaviour happening. Variables such as who was present, and differences to routine, contextual information (such as a visit by a relative, change of school) that created an emotional upset should be included. Avoid making assumptions.

Behaviour – This is the action or actions which you want to find an explanation for. Therefore it is important to describe the distressed behaviour as precisely as possible. Can you include information about the frequency, intensity or duration of your child's behaviour? (In other words how long the behaviour lasted, how many times the behaviour occurred. The intensity of the behaviour should include detail such as did the behaviour cause bruising, break the skin.)

Consequences – This is an event, object or situation which occurs immediately after or shortly after the distressed behaviour and has an influence on whether or not that behaviour occurs again on a similar occasion in the future. Examples include consequences which are known to reinforce behaviour such as pleasant attention (cuddling); other kinds of attention which most people do not find reinforcing but your child may such as speaking in an angry tone; attention from other children; noise (such as that resulting from head banging or chair throwing) and escape.

> Daniel is taken to his cousin's birthday party. When he arrives he runs into the utility room and sits on the floor. His mum tries to coax him out; he screams and bites his hand; his mum returns to the kitchen.

Antecedent: What causes the behaviour	Daniel's mum tries to remove him from the utility room
Behaviour: What the individual does	Daniel screams and bites his hand
Consequences: What happens as a result	Mum withdraws

The function of this behaviour is social avoidance. Daniel has learned that if he screams and bites his hand his mum will withdraw. But we also have to ask why did he not want to be in the party? The probable cause was Daniel's inability to cope with such a noisy, socially demanding environment. By not understanding that the party was too much for Daniel his mum has created a situation for Daniel to learn a negative behaviour.

Antecedents and consequences can make a behaviour more or less likely to occur. In the following example it is the consequence that makes Alex's behaviour more likely to occur in the future.

Antecedent: What causes the behaviour	Alex was sitting watching TV in the front room. His sister Penny walks in and changes the channel to a programme she wants to watch.
Behaviour: What the individual does	Alex got up and walked over to Penny and kicked her.
Consequences: What happens as a result	Penny started to cry. Mum came into the room and told Penny to go and play in her room. Alex was left alone to watch TV.

The function of this behaviour is to be left alone and to be able to watch the TV programme that he wanted to watch. Alex has learned that if he kicks his sister his mum will take her out of the room.

A lot of behaviours are learned and therefore they can in time, if necessary, become unlearned. But we also have to understand the demands we put on our children may sometimes be too much for them to handle. By putting them in situations they find distressing we may actually be forcing them to use negative behaviours as a reaction.

Using the ABC approach it may be possible to identify that if a distressed behaviour occurs as a result of a particular antecedent or consequence, the distressed behaviour can be decreased by changing those influences. This approach therefore aims to *increase appropriate behaviours* by using antecedents and consequences which make them more likely to occur again and by reinforcing consequences which make the appropriate behaviour more likely to occur again. This approach therefore aims to *decrease inappropriate or distressed behaviours* by using your knowledge of the antecedents and/or consequences to make the behaviour less likely to occur again.

Changing behaviours

Many parents come to us asking us for help in changing the behaviours that they see as unacceptable in their children. But do all distressed behaviours need to be fixed? What if some of those behaviours are so crucial to the individual that by trying to suppress them we may actually be making the behaviours worse? We also personally feel that it shows a lack of respect for the individual with autism if we do not acknowledge just how important some behaviours are to them.

Changing behaviour is often time consuming and difficult with quite frankly limited results. We also attempt to change behaviours before we have even learned to manage them. If we take those behaviours labelled as obsessions or ritualistic or self-stimulating, for instance, they may serve a purpose either in maintaining equilibrium or making the world predictable for them. Spinning and rocking has always been seen as a behaviour to eradicate. Well, actually when Linda sees her son in the swimming pool spinning in the water with an ecstatic look on his face she thinks why would she want to stop that? It is far better to make the behaviours manageable for all concerned.

Christopher had an obsession with drinking straws, the ones with the bendy bit at the top; he went through dozens every day and would then post them. Linda and her husband found them under furniture, behind radiators, stuffed in the air conditioning vents in the car, in the video player, stuffed down the overflow in the sink and even in the toilet cistern! Linda's strategy was to put them out of sight and try and limit them. She felt torn as she didn't want to not give them to him as she could see they served a very important purpose in that by twizzling the straw in front of his eyes Christopher enjoyed the visual stimulus and the constant twizzling seemed to calm him down when he was anxious. Linda became the keeper of the straws and Christopher became more and more agitated when Linda wasn't quick enough in getting them from the cupboard often leading to him lashing out at her. Eventually she realized that because of his autism he needed to visually see that there was always a straw available when he might need it so Linda and her husband purchased a straw dispenser where you lift the lid and the straws pop up. They placed it on the work top and pointed it out to Christopher. He emptied it in a few seconds and so they refilled it. They continued to do this all day as he pulled them out in a frenzy. By the second day he had slowed down as it began to dawn on him that the straws were always going to be there when he needed them. By the end of the week he was down to 8–10 straws a day. Not only was the straw situation much more manageable but he had also learned self-regulation. They had managed the behaviour, not changed it.

Self-injurious behaviour

Self-injurious behaviour is not uncommon in individuals with ASD. It can be very distressing for parents to witness this behaviour and many parents report that this is one of the hardest things they have to cope with. Suffice to say that if your child is hurting themselves, whether intentionally or not

– this is self-injurious behaviour. It may include biting self, pulling own hair out, head banging, face slapping, kicking and punching self, or knocking body against hard surfaces.

Some self-injurious behaviours can go on for a long time. There are reports of individuals who have been self-injuring for many years. But these may be unusual people, with very extreme self-injury. What we do know is that the more serious the self-injury, the more long lasting it seems to be. We also know that self-injurious behaviours can come and go throughout an individual's life and the teenage years can be particularly difficult.

It can be influenced by environmental factors and physical health. As we have mentioned before we need to find out the function of the behaviour. It may be that the individual's communication skills are poor and they have learned that if they hurt themselves people come and pay attention to them, or it maybe they have learned that people go away when they do it. We then have to try and help the individual communicate their needs and wants in a more positive way. The behaviour can mean different things at different times and so it can be very difficult to work out what the message is. Again careful observation and keeping a diary (perhaps using the ABC approach) can be useful. They may engage in this behaviour when they are stressed, or bored. They may be in physical pain; for example, hitting their face constantly could be a sign of tooth pain. It may be due to sensory issues which should also be investigated.

Jane says:

> My daughter would bite her hand all the time and she had terrible calluses and it was really distressing. An occupational therapist carried out a sensory assessment and she suggested we get her a bite ring as she may have been seeking sensory feedback in her jaw. We went to the pet

shop and found a puppy toy that was pink (her favourite colour) and we tied pink ribbon around it. She carried it round with her and would bite on it when ever she needed to. It stopped her biting her hand and since then we have thought of other ways to help her, such as eating crunchy food and chewing gum.

In cases where the self-injury is serious and prolonged, medication may be considered. The suggestion is that either the constant and prolonged injury leads to the individual producing an increased level of endorphins which work in the same way as morphine to deaden the pain or that they become addicted to the 'high' produced by the endorphins and therefore sustain the behaviour. The usual medication used is called naltrexone. It acts to block the production of the endorphins and it can help reduce the behaviours while the medication is in use. This has been found to be beneficial in some cases but must be used under strict medical and psychological supervision and is only used in extreme cases.

Helping your child

- Always check out if the self-injurious behaviour is due to an underlying physical health issue.

- Teach communication skills, using pictures, gestures, signs, etc., whichever is appropriate to your child.

- Make sure your child is not in danger but try not to react to the behaviour. If this is their way of communicating the need for a drink make sure you pre-empt this by offering them a drink more frequently.

- Coping with self-injurious behaviour alone is stressful and because of its complexity we really need to know why the behaviours are occurring; seeking out professional help is crucial.

- Keep a first aid kit handy so that you do not have to worry about infections.

Linda says:

Christopher's self-injury started at the same time as his physical aggression toward others. We looked at when Christopher was likely to self-injure; low mood, anxiety, too much unstructured time, frustration due to the communication difficulties and our response and reaction to behaviours all impacted on him. We learned to recognize the signs, e.g. anxious questioning, withdrawal. We also looked at ways of pre-empting the eruptions. We looked at how we lived and made the changes to our environment, our routine and the way we communicated. We worked as a team offering him the consistency and structure that is so important to anyone with autism.

Having addressed some of the more urgent issues we began to look more closely at the whole area of self-injury and we had been focusing on the way Christopher hurt himself when he was upset but we had not really looked at the fact that he was also hurting himself seemingly unintentionally and we hadn't really understood the impact of his sensory difficulties. Firm massage and gentle singing had always calmed Christopher down and we knew that he had sensory issues in that he found certain sounds and tones distressing, but then I began to read in more depth about the impact sensory difficulties had on people with autism. Much has been written but I found Olga Bogdashina (2003) very useful. She looks at how sensory perceptual difficulties affect the behaviour of people with autism. We began to identify the areas where Christopher had problems and at last had some more answers to why he hurt himself either intentionally or as a consequence of his sensory difficulties. His need for deep pressure was obvious and he would try and squeeze between the bed and the wall. He would bang his leg against the radiator and press his head back against the headboard. We started to put the strategies in place suggested by her, for example building in to his timetable regular deep massage. We used his love of the great outdoors to implement a regular physical activity programme and we certainly kept the opportunity for sensory overload to an absolute minimum. This combined with all our other strategies to keep his anxiety levels as low as possible have all had a beneficial effect.

Christopher is a very complex character: the causes of his behaviours are not always easy to unpick, nor do we have all the answers, but by understanding how he experiences the world through his senses and how these senses can become 'distorted' by his autism, we feel better able to reduce some of the self-injurious behaviours.

Sleeping problems

There is nothing more likely to make life difficult to tolerate than lack of sleep. Many children with ASD have chronic or recurring sleep problems and many parents report that their child sleeps in their bed with them at night. This is not unusual with typically developing toddlers, but it seems that with some of our children this is going on for a much longer period of time. Many parents have reported that their children are still sharing their bed into their teenage years and beyond.

Parents tend not to seek help as they are often embarrassed to admit their 14-year-old son is still getting into their bed.

Jeff says:

> We regularly play 'musical beds'. My son Jack will not go to bed on his own so one of us lies beside him while he goes off; this can take a couple of hours. Then it seems no sooner are we in bed than he comes into us and we are so tired I usually go into his bed just to get some sleep so I can function at work the next day. I don't think my wife and I have slept together all night for at least ten years. We have tried on several occasions to stop it but we all get so tired and grouchy it just doesn't seem worth it.

Using medication to sedate our children at night time may be tempting but the long-term detrimental effects of the use of hypnotics (sleeping tablets) are well documented.

However, another treatment that has become popular over the last few years is *melatonin*. This is a naturally occurring hormone secreted by the pineal gland in humans and animals. We all need to have adequate levels of melatonin in our blood in order to ensure a good night's sleep. It works by regulating our circadian rhythms (sleep patterns). It has been popular in some countries for several years to alleviate the symptoms of jet lag. Many parents have reported that it works well for their child; some also report that it has no effect. As it is a naturally occurring hormone, few adverse side effects have been reported, but more research is needed. It is not available over the counter in the UK and we would advise you to speak to your doctor if you think this may help.

Dr David Bramble (1997) is a psychiatrist with a special interest in ASD and sleep. He carried out research into sleep problems in children with development delay and found that after a two-week behavioural modification treatment plan there was a 59 per cent reduction in night time awakenings and all the parents in the trial reported that their children settled more quickly and were less distressed. In a follow-up study 18 months later all but three of the 15 children no longer had any sleep-related problems. Dr Bramble regularly puts on sleep workshops for parents and many have reported that this method works well. Dr Bramble recommends the following treatment plan.

Ten steps to a quiet night with children:

1. Make the bedroom safe, secure and unstimulating – remember your child may be overloaded by bright colour or loud and patterned wallpaper curtains and duvets.

2. Set regular bedtime and waking time and stick to it.

3. Avoid stimulating activities (rough play, loud music, TV) in the hour before bedtime.

4. Have a pre-bedtime settling routine (use symbols, pictures, timers).

5. Have a rapid settling routine in the bedroom; lights off; door closed.

6. Ignore the child thereafter (unless physically unwell). Put them back without fuss if he/she gets up during the night (don't talk at all).

7. Don't give in – you will only train your child to get worse if you do!

8. Praise and cuddle (if tolerated) once awake in the morning following a good night.

9. There will be initial worsening of the problem. That means it is working.

10. Stick to this and your child will learn not to disturb you in the night.

Be careful to plan:

1. Choose a good time for the whole family (no holidays, special events, other children's exam times).

2. Make sure you are all in good health.

3. Be prepared to move bedroom furniture/change bedrooms especially if it is known that they sleep in other houses such as grandma's or respite.

4. Support and encourage other children whilst this programme is being followed.

5. Discuss progress with a friend, family member or professional.

6. Warn neighbours of temporary disruption and noise.

7. If possible brief your child thoroughly before and throughout the plan.

8. Wavering parents need to back each other up.

9. If illness is suspected pause until they are well again.

10. Persist and it stands a good chance of working in three to four nights.

Ideas for a graded withdrawal for a child who insists on staying in your room:

1. Place mattress on floor next to the bed and switch the bedroom light off.

2. Lie next to your child on the bed for three nights.

3. Lie on the mattress next to the bed for three nights.

4. Move the mattress by two feet closer to the door every three nights.

5. When at the door sit on a chair in the bedroom with the door open for three nights.

6. Sit on a chair outside the room but visible to the child with the door open for three nights.

7. Sit on a chair outside the room not visible to the child with the door open for three nights.

8. Sit on a chair outside the bedroom with the door closed for three nights.

NB: If your child tries to join you return them to their bed with no fuss and no eye contact.

This method is not for the faint hearted – it will take an enormous amount of willpower and energy on your part, but given the effect lack of sleep and not spending your nights in bed with your partner can have on relationships we think it may be worth it. If however it all seems too much to cope with at the moment then you need to relax about your family's sleeping arrangements and take comfort from the fact that by the time they are adults most of your children will be sleeping in their own beds!

Dealing with emerging sexuality

Explaining what sexuality and relationships is all about to someone who has a problem relating to other people and poor understanding of social rules can be extremely difficult, but it is a crucial part of your child's development. It is especially important for those more able children who are likely to be mixing with their typically developing peers. We will revisit this more fully in Chapter 7.

Mention the word masturbation at a parent support group and those parents of younger children quite often look panic stricken, especially as the parents of older children start comparing notes about their most embarrassing moments with their children's sexual development. Some parents may find it difficult to accept their child's changing sexual identity and needs. Although a child with ASD may be intellectually and emotionally far behind his typically developing peers, his physical development will not be delayed.

How we view masturbation will be dictated by our individual value and belief system related to sexuality. Mostly it is viewed as healthy and normal and for a lot of individuals with ASD it is likely to be their only sexual outlet. We just need to teach them where and when it is appropriate. Rather than trying to tell or show them where they shouldn't masturbate it is much more effective to tell them where they can. The most obvious is their own private space of their bedroom.

Linda says:

I remember when Christopher started to fondle himself and get an erection. I thought it was going to be really difficult to get him to understand that he couldn't do it whilst sitting on the sofa. But after leading him upstairs to his bedroom a few times as soon as he started he quickly learned what to do. Eventually I was just able to say 'In your bedroom, Chris' as soon as he started and he would go. Now he just goes to his bedroom whenever he becomes aroused.

Just like the rest of the population what makes an individual sexually aroused can differ widely for individuals with ASD and some parents have felt shocked and embarrassed by their son or daughter's sexual preferences.

Case study

One parent contacted us in a very distressed state. Her son John is 14 years old and has Asperger Syndrome. She had found a number of disposable nappies under his bed; he had obviously ejaculated into them. She was shocked and removed them and told him he shouldn't do it any more. Some days later he was caught stealing some from the shelf in the supermarket. Again she became upset with him and told him it was wrong to steal. John become very upset and angry. A few weeks later he was arrested as he had been found on the floor of the baby changing room with his trousers down and ejaculating into a nappy. He was cautioned and referred to a psychologist.

We reassured his mother that this sort of behaviour was not unusual and that it was much better to make the nappies available to John so that he could meet his sexual need in the privacy of his own bedroom, which is what he was doing in the first place rather than putting himself at risk by doing it in a public place. Although this was difficult for her she agreed that it was the best thing to do.

Helping your child

- Be prepared and be careful how you respond to the behaviour which is a natural part of growing up.

- Use pictures or symbols to help your child understand appropriate time and place.

- Don't be afraid to seek help from professionals and other parents; remember you are not the only parent to have faced these problems.

Chapter 3

The Low Arousal Approach

Low arousal'

The low arousal approach is the cornerstone of the Studio III method of managing distressed behaviour. The approach gives a framework for managing your child. It is an approach which, in some ways, is counterintuitive in that it goes against most of the rules we have for parenting children and young people. It starts with us looking how we operate around the young person. It questions all our assumptions and examines our values and beliefs, and forces us to look inward and take control of the way we react and respond to distressed behaviour. Therefore, it does not come easy. It is worth persevering; remember, it is a skill like any other and therefore it has to be practised!

From experience, both personal and working with families, most of the conflict comes from differences of opinion on how to handle and react to the distressed behaviour our children have. As we have said before we cannot stress too strongly the importance of working as a team: only by supporting each other and having a consistent approach can we make progress. Do you recognize some of the following beliefs?

'He should be "made" to understand when he has done something wrong.'

'It's not fair on the other children that he who challenges takes up the most of our time.'

'I shouldn't let him get away with it.'

'If I back down then I will have lost face and will not be able to assert myself in the future.'

'I shouldn't let him win.'

'She knows exactly what she is doing.'

'I shouldn't give him what he wants because it is rewarding distressed behaviour.'

'She shouldn't behave like this.'

It's easy to get stuck in these feeling of annoyance, anger and
resentment. We are not advocating that our children should
just be allowed to do as they wish; it's just that we need to
change the way we think about how we manage them. It is
important to understand that the goal of short-term behaviour management is to keep everyone safe and that will likely
mean not making a stand or being confrontational and may
mean backing off and walking away. The longer-term work on
teaching our children self-control, anger management, social
skills, etc., goes on but *not* when they are in a state of crisis, or,
as we will refer to this state, arousal. People do not learn any
lessons when they are in this state.

It can't be stressed strongly enough the effect that high
levels of arousal have on the behaviour of our children and
young people. When we are frightened we experience what
can be referred to as 'the flight or fight response', which is an
adaptive response left over from when early man really did
have to respond quickly in the presence of danger. It prepares
the body to either stand and fight or to run away as quickly
as possible. When we feel we are in danger proteins such as
adrenalin are released in our bodies and our frontal lobe (the
part of the brain that acts as an inhibitor of our actions) starts
to shut down. Our limbic system takes over and our brain
does three things – we freeze, locate the problem and then
decide either to flight or fight. As the limbic system takes
over our hearing shuts down, as does our peripheral vision;
everything we do now is reactive.

To understand this is to understand what happens when our children reach crisis point. We also need therefore to realize that to try and reason with someone in this state or to put demands on them to 'calm down' are futile; instead we should be making sure that we are confident and calm and able to distract, redirect or remove either the source of their anxiety or remove them from that source. Maintaining our state of calmness is incredibly important as if our arousal levels are as high as theirs then that means that all the physiological changes happening to them are also happening to us and we become very reactive rather than being able to think clearly.

Everything we do should be geared to reducing arousal levels and making the world as safe and predictable as we can – we reduce the anxiety, arousal levels reduce and then incidents of distressed behaviour reduce.

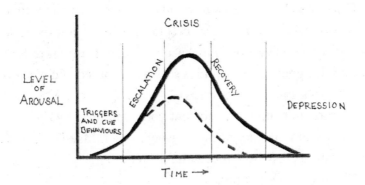

Understanding the effects of arousal

As you can see the level of arousal rises over time as your child may become distressed. This may be caused by *triggers* which may be unique to your child such as sensory overload, fear, anxiety, too many demands, tiredness, and ill health. You need to be able to recognize and understand these triggers in order to reduce them, remove them or remove your child from them. There is only a small window of opportunity to do this; by this we mean *time* before your child reaches the point of no return (*crisis*). Strategies may include distracting, redirecting or removing your child.

Sometimes we cannot see the triggers as they may be internal to your child; therefore we need to be able to recognize how their behaviour is changing (this is called *cue behaviours*). It may be pacing, shouting, self-injury, rocking, humming, increased questions.

If we do not recognize and deal with the situation at this point things will *escalate* quite quickly and your child will go into *crisis*. Remember this is not the time to reason or remonstrate; all we can do now is make sure that your child and yourselves are safe.

Once the crisis appears to be over, we need to allow time for *recovery* which may take several hours. This is not the time to ask for an apology or to make any demands or reintroduce the initial trigger as your child is still very aroused and may go straight back into another crisis.

All too often after any incident your child may be *depressed* afterwards and may cry or become very quiet. Make sure they have a safe space where they can recover.

The low arousal approach is:

- A non-confrontational way of managing challenging behaviour.

- A philosophy of care which is based on valuing the individual.

- An approach that specifically attempts to avoid aversive interventions (such as reprimands, punishment such as 'smacking' your child's hand when they do something wrong; in the long distant past aversive intervention such as using a fine mist of water at room temperature would be sprayed on a child's face to stop any distressed behaviours; thankfully research has proven that this type of intervention – introducing something unwelcome and perhaps unpleasant – may not help in reducing behaviours).

- An approach that requires us to focus on our own responses and behaviour and not just locate the problem with the individual with ASD.

- A collection of strategies that are designed to rapidly reduce aggression.

It is based upon the following assumptions:

Assumption One: Most individuals who are distressed are usually extremely aroused at the time. Therefore, we should avoid doing things that will further arouse your child who is probably already upset.

Assumption Two: A large proportion of distressed behaviours are usually preceded by demands/requests. Therefore, reducing these demands or requests should help to defuse incidents.

Assumption Three: Most common communication is predominately non-verbal rather than verbal. Therefore, we should be aware of the signals that we communicate when they are upset.

'Don't pour fuel on the fire'

Any individual who is threatening or aggressive can be extremely frightening. Often the responses we give tend to increase their behaviour until something extreme happens.

A commonplace observation is that it is difficult to reason with an individual who does not wish to be reasoned with.

When they are upset or angry, what we do or say or what we don't do or don't say could have an effect on the situation we are trying to manage.

We recommend the following interpersonal rules to promote a positive engagement approach to managing any incident. (We explore this further in Chapter 4 with a photograph to illustrate these rules.)

Appear calm

We know that trying to stay calm in a tense situation can be difficult. But if we can try to appear calm in these times, this may lead our children to feeling less confrontational.

To achieve this, we need to think of our body language:

Avoid tensing muscles, such as folding arms or clenching fists.

Breathe slowly and regularly.

Trying to appear calm on the outside when you are scared on the inside takes practice.

Personal space

Try to maintain a safe distance between you and your child when they are aroused. The minimum acceptable distance is approximately three feet.

At this distance, you can communicate with your child without 'invading' their space. If you have to back away to achieve this, do so in an unhurried manner.

Also moving towards your child at these times can be seen as threatening.

Eye contact

Sustained eye contact (staring) is an almost universal sign for aggression in the animal world. Avoid staring at your child when they are aroused, but do try and maintain regular inter-mittent eye contact.

If you find this difficult, look somewhere else on their face, for example their forehead.

Touch

Touch is generally perceived by people as either a sign of warmth and friendliness or as a signal of dominance.

Even though you know your child well, always avoid touching them when they are aroused, at least initially.

When they appear to be calming down, it may well be appropriate to touch them, but be aware that they may not interpret this contact in the manner which you intended it.

Noise

When your child is upset, the noises that surround them can make a situation worse. So think of the environment: turn the radio or television down or off.

Listen

Listen to what your child is saying as they are often trying to tell you something. It may well be something very simple that is upsetting them and can be sorted out just by talking about it.

It is often a good idea to try sitting your child down to talk to them. But remember your body language and personal space so do not sit too close to them and do not stand over them. Sit or kneel at a safe distance.

Communication

How we communicate with people is very important at any time, more so when your child is upset. Be aware of tone of voice. Speak slowly, calmly, and softly.

Keep your sentences short and simple. Using overlong sentences or explanations can make your child more confused. Do not argue with them.

Non-verbal communication

Again, be aware of your body language; avoid arms folded and appearing distracted. Ensure you show the individual that they have your complete attention (for example stop what you were doing and look toward your child).

Distract

Opportunities to distract often present themselves. Try to change the subject (avoid being obvious about this) and talk about things and subjects that your child likes.

Be aware if you promise your child something you are morally obliged to provide it, so for example do not promise to take them somewhere later if it is not possible to do so.

Remove other people

To avoid an escalating situation consider removing other people from the area. It is a lot easier to remove these people than trying to remove the individual who is upset.

This approach really is the most effective way of working: it's not always easy to achieve, it does take practice, it really does challenge all our instincts around managing behaviour and it does take team work, sometimes we get it wrong, we are not machines but we learn from it and move on! This low arousal approach though is not just for dealing with a crisis; it needs to be a way of life.

Linda says:

We have applied it to our living environment, our expectations of Christopher, in fact anything we can control. We do not put pressure on him which we know he may not be able to cope with. If that means one of us missing a family celebration or trip then so be it. We have a rule in our house: nobody shouts unless the house is on fire! We do not enter into heated discussions or argument when he is around (this rule also applies to visitors!) and we try to keep the atmosphere as calm as possible at all times. When we know that Christopher's arousal levels are high we will always back off and leave him to calm down in his own time. We no longer worry what others think; everyone is welcome in our house but they have to abide by the low arousal rules whenever Christopher is home. I know that this is not easy for a lot of families given that there may be more than one child involved but it is useful just to stand back and look at how the family operates and where changes can be made.

The wrong way – pouring fuel on the fire	The right way – the low arousal approach
Mum: Nazreen, can you put your washing away?	*Mum: Nazreen, can you put your washing away?*
Nazreen: No, you do it.	*Nazreen: No, you do it.*
Mum: No, you need to do it.	*Mum: No, you need to do it.*
Nazreen: No, you do it.	*Nazreen: No, you do it.*
Mum: It's on your programme, you need to do it.	*Mum: It's on your programme, you need to do it.*
Nazreen: No, you do it.	*Nazreen: No, you do it.*
Nazreen starts to bite her hand.	Nazreen starts to bite her hand.
Mum: Stop that and anyway the school said you MUST do it.	*Mum: Nazreen, tell you what, shall I carry the basket to your room and when WE have put your clothes away we can watch that video.*
Nazreen: No, you do it. I don't want to. Nazreen starts to hit her head against the wall.	Mum picks up basket and walks out of room.
Mum: What am I supposed to tell school?	Nazreen follows.
Nazreen takes the washing basket and throws it at mum.	

You may feel that this is 'giving in', but remember our goal is to avoid a crisis and keep everybody safe. When Nazreen is calm and happy mum may ask Nazreen why she got upset. It may be that she was not feeling well, that there were more clothes in the basket than she was used to, that at school she had a drink break between tasks. We always need to try and find out what the triggers are. When Nazreen is calm and happy mum may attempt this again.

The wrong way – pouring fuel on the fire	The right way – the low arousal approach
Sonia: You need to turn that off. I want to watch my programme now.	*Sonia: You need to turn that off. I want to watch my programme now.*
Noah: No.	*Noah: No.*
Sonia: I want to watch my programme now. It's not fair; you always have what you want on.	*Sonia: I want to watch my programme now. It's not fair; you always have what you want on.*
Noah: No.	*Noah: No.*
Noah starts to hit his leg with the remote.	Noah starts to hit his leg with the remote.
Sonia shouts: It's not fair, I'm going to tell mum.	*Sonia shouts: It's not fair, I'm going to tell mum.*
Mum: Noah, let your sister watch her programme. I am sick of Doctor Who anyway.	*Mum: Tell you what, Sonia, where's your comic? I am sure there is something about horses in there that we could look at together.*
Sonia goes to take the remote from Noah.	
Noah snatches it back and throws it at his mother.	

Again, you may feel that this approach is not fair. But remember this is a short-term option. In the long term we need to look at strategies for managing Noah's obsession with Doctor Who such as time limits or his own TV. In this instance, mum used her distraction techniques with Sonia.

Creating a low arousal environment

This is not just about the physical environment but also the emotional environment we live in. This includes for a time removing any precious ornaments, etc., that you have, and perhaps not having too much noise in the house (for example the TV on in one room, a radio in another). Arguments and heated discussions should also not take place within your child's hearing. If at all possible let your child with ASD have their own bedroom as they will need a safe space where they can escape to when they are feeling stressed. Keep the décor neutral as bright colours and heavy patterns may be too much for your child. Put loose covers on the furniture, rugs on the floor, laminate floor instead of carpet — so that you can relax in your home and not worry about any damage. This will reduce your own anxiety and arousal levels as well as your child's.

Going with the flow and being less uptight about things really is quite liberating! Go on take time out! / relax!

CHAPTER 4

Using Video

Having learned more about the importance of your own reactions and the importance of low arousal, we now want to take you through some practical steps which may help you manage your son or daughter's behaviour. But first you must leave behind your assumptions that include the belief that your child:

- is attention seeking

- is trying to annoy you

- is trying to upset you

- has bad manners

- is behaving in a way that demonstrates that you are a bad parent/a reflection that you are not in control

- must learn to behave

- or that you must stop their behaviour in order to protect your child.

It is important to look at your assumptions about your child's behaviour as we know from Dave Dagnan's studies that when care staff make judgements of responsibility for challenging behaviour there is a link to the emotional and helping responses they give. As yet though, the researcher has not used the same studies with parents. Part of Dave Dagnan's Thoughts About Challenging Behaviour Questionnaire (2007) is included at the end of this chapter (remember it is written for care staff to fill in), but we think you may find the results surprising if you fill it in for yourselves (or get each family member to fill it in and then share your results – there is a good chance that you all have different thoughts about how responsible your child is for their distressed behaviour).

Andy McDonnell in the Foreword to this book writes that video is a powerful tool and that it may also help you describe to professionals what difficulties they often experience. We would caution you from using video as a means of demonstrating what you have to 'go through or put up with'. This suggests that you don't believe that the professional understands your situation and that your situation is far worse than they can imagine or have ever come across before. Using video is a concept that you may be feeling anxious about – as you may be feeling self-conscious. Funnily enough most families that Andrea has worked with initially feel the same and are hesitant when the word video is suggested. But after a trial run families seem to forget that they are on camera and find the experience cathartic.

Jackie says:

> When Andrea said she wanted to video me I thought she was joking. I had been watching Big Brother and the Video Diaries programmes on telly and could not understand how all these people could forget about the camera, be talking to the camera and opening up...saying things straight from their heart. Then she brought the camera. At first I was thinking I wished I had had my hair done and should I change out of my slippers! And then I just forgot

it was there…Andrea was asking me to describe what my daughter did and to tell her how it made me feel…and that's what I did… I felt some kind of release…I just told her and the camera…when I watched the tape the following week it made me think…listening to myself made all the information I had been given make sense for the first time in 30 years…and I did it…I changed my reaction when Cathy walked in the kitchen when I was cooking her dinner and instead of me shouting at her in panic to get out of my way just in case she touched the pan (which always resulted in her shouting and making a grab at me), I looked at her and said 'Dinner's nearly ready, can you set the table'…she smiled at me and said 'Yes'…and that was that.

Mita says:

I used the video as a way of getting us all to communicate with each other. We all talked to the camera about Arfan, me, my mum, Arfan's sister and my husband. Then when Arfan was at respite we all sat down together and watched each other's video. Listening to my husband was the most surprising; I did not know he felt that way.

Another way to check what assumptions you have is to video yourselves in the following situation:

You will need at least two people (or three people): you (playing yourself), a member of your family/a friend/a professional (playing the role of your child) and if possible someone to switch the video camera on/off.

You will need a video camera and a tripod – line this up so that you can capture the following on film:

Write down the distressed situations that you have to manage (this is like a script to keep you on task).

Then, on video – describe the behaviour that your son/daughter displays and what you do – then role play to camera (try if possible to film in the house where the behaviour takes place, such as by the TV, by the front door).

After each behaviour – talk on camera about how this behaviour makes you feel (this is very important) and what you think about your son/daughter when they are doing these things.

Take a break – ideally overnight – then watch this film – were there any surprises? Are you responding in a positive way/are you making things worse? Under stress are you making assumptions which are not there when you are calm, relaxed, in control?

Look at the film again – can you put any of the low arousal principles into place?

Now look at your body language/your posture – are you relaxed/stressed? Could your body language be interpreted by your son/daughter as aggressive?

What about your voice when you are responding to your son/daughter's behaviour – does it sound harsh/stressed/aggressive/confrontational? Often when we are advising parents and professional carers about managing situations, our first piece of advice is to tell them to be quiet – not to say anything at these times – as it is often difficult to manage a situation which you find frightening/distressed. Remember to be calm and try and sound calm and relaxed at the same time *and* remember to match your body language up to these thoughts.

Now look at the video again in terms of your body language – do you look calm and in control? If not, here's some tips.

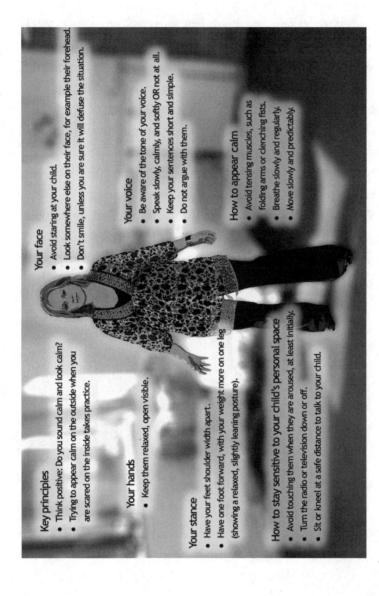

Key principles

- Think positive: Do you sound calm and look calm?
- Trying to appear calm on the outside when you are scared on the inside takes practice.

Your hands

- Keep them relaxed, open visible.

Your stance

- Have your feet shoulder width apart.
- Have one foot forward, with your weight more on one leg (showing a relaxed, slightly leaning posture).

How to stay sensitive to your child's personal space

- Avoid touching them when they are aroused, at least initially.
- Turn the radio or television down or off.
- Sit or kneel at a safe distance to talk to your child.

Your face

- Avoid staring at your child.
- Look somewhere else on their face, for example their forehead.
- Don't smile, unless you are sure it will defuse the situation.

Your voice

- Be aware of the tone of your voice.
- Speak slowly, calmly, and softly OR not at all.
- Keep your sentences short and simple.
- Do not argue with them.

How to appear calm

- Avoid tensing muscles, such as folding arms or clenching fists.
- Breathe slowly and regularly.
- Move slowly and predictably.

Key principles

Over the next few weeks put all these new thoughts and body language into action and *when you are ready video yourself again – exactly as before.*

As before, take a break – ideally overnight – then watch this film. Now compare your responses.

Were there any surprises this time? Are you responding in a positive way/are you making things worse? If you were stressed the first time, are you less stressed now?

Looking at the film again – have you put any of the low arousal principles into place?

Now look at your body language/your posture – are you relaxed/stressed? Can you make any more changes?

What about your voice when you are responding to your son/daughter's behaviour – have you managed to stay quiet? Are you happy with what you are seeing – are there any other changes that you can make?

The thoughts about challenging behaviour questionnaire

Listed below are the thoughts that people may have when dealing with a person who presents with challenging behaviour. Think about challenging behaviour that you have experienced from a client recently. For each thought please put a tick in the box that shows how much you agree with each statement.

	Agree strongly	Agree slightly	Unsure	Disagree slightly	Disagree strongly
He/she is trying to wind me up					
He/she can't help him/herself					
He/she is doing it deliberately					
He/she knows what he/she is doing					
He/she has no control over his/her behaviour					
He/she could stop if he/she wanted					
He/she is trying to manipulate the situation					
He/she can think through his/her actions					
He/she does not mean to upset people					
He/she is in control of his/her behaviour					
He/she means to make me feel bad					
He/she has chosen to behave in this way					
He/she is not to blame for what they do					
He/she knows the best time to challenge					
He/she does not realize how it makes me feel					

CHAPTER 5

Relationships: Keeping It Together!

Relationships

There are many books, articles and internet sites looking at autism and aspects of relationships between parents and professionals. This chapter is not research based – it is a collection of our experiences, supported by colleagues, our friends and people we have met, with ideas to help you develop a greater relationship with your child and each other.

Good relationships in the family

Being part of a family with a child with distressed behaviour can be very difficult. We know that statistically more marriages fail where there is a child with a disability as the strain on relationships is immense. Emotions such as grief, anger, resentment and sadness and feelings of isolation are not uncommon.

Below are some individual stories which you may identify with.

Carol's story

My grandson Joel is now 19 years old. My husband and I live quite close to our son and his wife and so when he was very little we spent a lot of time with him. He was diagnosed as autistic when he was three. As you can imagine we were all devastated. We tried to be supportive, but the more we read the more guilt we felt; they said there was a genetic link and so we felt somehow we were to blame. We helped out whenever we could although he was a real handful. The older he got, the more unpredictable his behaviour became and their visits became fewer. By the time he turned 13 he became physically aggressive and we witnessed several incidents when he attacked his parents. We felt so helpless, we really couldn't manage him on our own and yet we knew they needed help. I think they were embarrassed and our relationship became very strained; we loved them both and we adored Joel but it seems everything we said or suggested was seen as a criticism. It was a very sad time for all of us; I know that they were grieving but we were too.

Grandparents are usually a great source of support and many families could not cope without their input but as Carol's story shows it's not always plain sailing. Sometimes we get so wrapped up in our own grief that we do not always recognize that grandparents are going through similar problems of grief and anger and guilt. Over recent years the important role of grandparents has become more widely recognized. There are now organizations who do offer support and advice specifically to grandparents. You will find all the details later in this book.

Sara's story

I am the eldest of five children. My sister Jenny was born next two years after me; apparently my mum says that they knew something was wrong with her from the minute she was born. She was diagnosed as autistic at the age of two. From then on I became responsible for my little sister; I was the one who was able to interpret what she was saying and I seemed able to calm her when she became distressed. I remember feeling an overwhelming sense of responsibility for Jenny and was very protective of her, but as I got older I resented the time I had to spend with her. Also, I hate to admit it, but I was embarrassed when my friends came round as she would scream all the time and she used to wear nappies and she would put her hands in them and smear faeces everywhere. When we became teenagers it got worse as Jenny started to hurt me physically; I got a fair number of injuries and had lots of bald patches where she pulled my hair. She started to board at a special school and life became easier, but then I really missed her and felt terribly guilty. I eventually married and had children of my own. Jenny was by now in a residential home and we tried on a few occasions to have her stay with us but she really couldn't cope with small children and she was very aggressive toward them and they were very scared of her, so these visits were unsuccessful. Recently my brother and I visited Jenny and she hit him full in the face, making his nose bleed. It really is distressing; you feel all sorts of emotions, anger, guilt, resentment and sadness. I am sometimes resentful toward my parents because I feel my childhood was stolen in a way by having to look after Jenny but then I feel guilty because I really do love her.

As we can see from Sara's story, being the sibling of an individual with ASD can be very challenging. These feelings of negativity and anger are not uncommon, nor is the guilt they then feel for having these emotions. As parents we may rely on our other children both physically and emotionally and sometimes we may fail to see the impact of the burden of responsibility that they bear.

Mary says:

We made a conscious decision not to send our son with Asperger Syndrome to the same school as his sister because we felt she needed to have a space where she wasn't always watching out for him or even being embarrassed by him. It was a difficult decision because I would have felt far less stressed about his school day if I knew she was there to keep an eye on him and made sure he got there and back OK but I don't regret the decision. They have a pretty good relationship (most of the time).

Although there is no such thing as a typical family, we do know that often family life becomes fragmented and disrupted, and doing things together becomes a rare occurrence. Parents often find themselves trying to split their time between their child with ASD and their other children; it is unsatisfactory all round. Siblings may react by becoming more demanding and they may display negative behaviours in a bid to get themselves heard. They may not reveal their worries and feelings in an attempt to 'protect' their parents who they see as already struggling to cope. Sometimes, as parents we may invest all our hopes and expectations into our children without disabilities. We need to be careful, though, as often this can be a burden for our children and the pressure of having to succeed and do well is too much to bear.

Helping siblings to cope

- Give siblings a life of their own. Also help them to mix with other children who have brothers or sisters with ASD so they can see they are not alone.

- Involve them in 'the team'. We often try to protect siblings and fail to understand that they know what the problems are. Honesty is really the best policy.

- Make sure they have time to be who they are, away from the child with ASD. If *you* are unable (at this time) to give them separate time enlist other relatives and friends.

- Make sure you build their self-esteem by seeing them as individuals and not as your child with ASD's sibling.

- Let them see that it is OK to express negative feelings by allowing them to 'sound off' without feeling guilty.

- Make sure that they do not feel that the burden of responsibility will be theirs in the future. We want siblings to be advocates for and overseers of care for our children with ASD in the future, not their hands-on carers.

Many parents that we come into contact with feel guilty about the burden their non-autistic children bear, but thankfully it seems that as a rule they grow up to be happy and well adjusted individuals. At a recent parent training course in Ireland a now 35-year-old sibling came along with his parents. There were other parents attending who had young children with ASD and were expressing their worries about the strain on their young siblings. This is what he told them:

> I remember several occasions when life seemed difficult for me. One time we went on holiday to Butlin's holiday resort and my brother relieved himself in the swimming pool. I thought I would die of embarrassment, but I got over it. Another time I was about 16 and brought my first girlfriend home to meet mum and dad and as I came in the front door my brother ran down the stairs as naked as a jay bird. I thought I might die with shame! Twenty years on and I can look back and laugh. I am now happily married with two children of my own and I want to say now that I feel I am a better person for having experienced life with my brother. I love him dearly and will always want to be involved in his life.

Yes, it is difficult living with ASD but perhaps we need reminding of the positives!

There is an organization called Sibs which young and older siblings can contact for support; details are at the end of this book.

John's story

When my son Jack was born I was over the moon – I was sure he was going to play rugby for England. It all started to go wrong when he was around two. He wasn't meeting his milestones and was very overactive and slept very little; we were exhausted. His speech was also delayed. He was eventually diagnosed as autistic when he was three. We were both stunned; I couldn't believe it, not my boy. Looking back I know I found it hard to accept and wasn't as supportive to my wife as I could have been, but I was so angry. I set about looking at every idea of a 'cure' I could find. I found it really difficult to relate to Jack as he became more and more distressed. I worked away a lot and I have to tell you I felt quite relieved when I left on a Monday for the week, but then I felt almost straight away a real sense of guilt. Jack seemed to experience huge rages and my wife was usually the target. I just didn't know what to do. I felt I should be solving the problem and we would argue about the best way of dealing with his behaviour. I know my wife didn't tell me everything that happened when I was away as she didn't like the way I reacted. We stopped talking about it and I began to feel really excluded although I expect she would say I excluded myself by being absent so often. The strain on our relationship began to tell and we split up for a while. I started to have Jack on my own for visits and that's when it really hit me just how difficult it was to manage on your own and I realized just what she had been going through. But it was still difficult for us to talk as she was very defensive and protective of Jack. We needed help, our home was being systematically destroyed, we didn't go anywhere or invite anyone over and we were exhausted. I suppose we were at the end of our tether before anyone intervened and we were given some respite. Jack was assessed as needing a residential school and I'm ashamed to say I was relieved. My wife strongly resisted the idea and again we were in conflict. Eventually she succumbed to the pressure and he went. Our relationship dipped again as she blamed me for not being supportive enough. I was so frustrated; I wished I could be like her but then was really resentful that she made me feel so guilty. Several years on things have settled down and we are rebuilding our relationship. I still feel that she thinks I was the weak one and there is an unspoken criticism between us sometimes but we are working on it.

The role of fathers in caring for a child with a disability has until recently not attracted much research; however, things are changing, as is the willingness for more men to seek out help and support. Contact a Family have specific information for fathers on their website.

Keeping your relationships together: the importance of talking about incidents (also known as debriefing)

Being able to talk about the way we feel is a necessary part of coping with stress and yet quite often we tend not to voice our feelings because we are just getting on with coping each day at a time. This is often referred to as the 'emotional rucksack' – that is, we have an emotional event and rather than deal with it we put it into our rucksack saying we'll deal with that later, and then another problem arises and those feelings get put into the rucksack also....and so on and so on until the rucksack becomes so heavy we get weighed down by it and it gets dropped and all the emotions spill out at once and then watch out!

When we train staff, it's pretty straightforward; we talk about debriefing with a trusted colleague, but when the incident happens in the family it's not so easy. Who do we debrief to? As we have mentioned already we often cannot talk about our feelings to our partners or our parents as we veer between trying to protect them and feeling angry and resentful towards each other. A lot of the fathers we have worked with say that their opportunities to debrief are few and far between. 'How do you open up a conversation at the office with "I watched my son beat up his mother last night"?' said one father on a recent course.

Linda's voice:

I expect as you're reading this book you can relate to at least one of these experiences. I know that the strain on us as a couple was immense and our relationship was tested to the limits. I was very scared that Christopher would not be able to stay with us and became very secretive about just how violent he could be. I was in turn resentful and angry with my husband for often what I interpreted as 'leaving me to it'. In more recent years since we have been able to reflect on this very sad time my husband has been able to tell me how awful he felt when I was being hurt. If it had been a stranger he would have known what to do but when it's your child it's not so easy; he realized that protecting me could mean hurting him. He also felt excluded as I seemed to be so in control. If only he had known how I really felt! We have come a long way over the last few years and we are now more able to talk about things openly without being judgemental – well, most of the time! This means we are acting as a team and I know it feels much better to be pulling together rather than in different directions. Life can still be difficult and all sorts of pressures continue to challenge us but we are just better able to support each other through it.

The rules to get you talking about incidents:

It is crucial though that we do somehow make and take opportunities for debriefing. And there are some 'rules' that we should follow.

DO SO AS SOON AS POSSIBLE

To avoid the pitfall of storing the emotion in the rucksack, you need to get rid of it as soon as possible. It takes just a few minutes to get the initial emotion out, so it's not going to take up too much of your time!

FACE TO FACE IF POSSIBLE

Obviously it is much better to be able to talk to someone when you can see them; if not then a phone call can be helpful.

CONFIDENTIAL AND COMFORTABLE

You need to feel comfortable with the person you choose to talk about something that is so personal and upsetting to you and you need to know that what you say will be treated confidentially.

ACTIVELY LISTEN

There is nothing worse than when you are pouring your inner feelings out to someone and they start looking at their watch or start packing their bag, etc. Remember this if you are chosen!

BE NON-JUDGEMENTAL

The thing to remember about debriefing our way is that it is not a time to offer solutions, say how you would have done things differently, to apportion blame or 'collude' with feelings of resentfulness, fear and anger, etc. We don't want you to fix things, just listen!

Good relationships with professionals

For some families, visits from professionals such as community nurses can be very stressful. Some families suffer from more stress than others and, more importantly, some families cope extremely well and appear to bounce back from challenging situations.

Those families who experience optimism or an uplift in their care giving have long lasting stress alleviating affects, such as experiencing success with your child or success with aspects of your role as a carer. By following the low arousal approach outlined in this book, you should gain the confidence, skills and knowledge to manage distressing behaviours in a positive uplifting way. This in turn will lead to you developing the resilience necessary to reduce any stress that you may experience and allow you to experience the uplifts and successes that come your way. For example after reading this book we hope that you will have the abilities:

- to select an appropriate strategy from the ones we recommend to fit the challenges your child has and your family circumstances

- to make sense out of what often appears to be unusual or 'not normal' conditions

- to recognize your own expertise, and

- to continually reappraise which strategies work for you.

It's usually the woman (mum) who is the main carer and, in our experience, women are usually able to identify a higher proportion of coping strategies than men, and use more problem-solving approaches until they find something that works for their child and family. It's important to remember here that if you are able to explain, teach, develop coping strategies and keep the family together then you are also able to use the same strategies with any professionals who come into your life. Remember John's story earlier in this chapter as the role of fathers in caring for a child with a disability has until recently not attracted much research, but Linda and I feel that this is changing and fathers do have an important (if sometimes different) role to play.

All professionals strive for good practice. Within learning disability services, nurses are still fighting to justify why they are nurses and what their role is. In 2007 the Department of Health published guidance on good practice for learning disability nurses. Three aspects stand out:

'The person must be at the centre of his/her care and be fully involved in all aspects of planning, care and treatment.'

'Recognising the contribution of family carers and providing support to them in their role is critical.'

'The role of the learning disability nurse should be the championing of people with disabilities and their families.'

This presents us with a problem; that is occasionally the views of parents and professionals differ. Parents often battle with professionals to encourage them to see their viewpoint, access to treatment was influenced by views of the professionals and non-compliance occurred when parents had a different view from professionals. This is probably due to there still being stereotypes and myths held by some parents and professionals alike. One common stereotype is that some parents 'overprotect their child, underestimate their child's potential and reject help from services when they are offered'. This can lead to the perception that the parent is aloof or difficult. Ros Jarvis (2000) writes that 'letting go' is a professional term and it means removing ourselves from our children's lives and not interfering with what the professionals want to do. She goes on to say that many parents have over the years written about their experiences and the hurt caused by professionals and the exhaustion they feel by the procedures professionals put them through. She writes that many parents view professional ideas with suspicion because they have lived through initiatives that they perceived failed their child or that the professional starts something and then departs for new pastures. Families don't leave; they pick up the pieces when professionals make mistakes. Therefore it is not surprising that parents are sceptical about professional help.

'Parenting competence' – where else but with a child with a disability do parents, professionals and researchers automatically question competence? Or that parents feel that professionals do not understand the pressures of parenting their child?

Many parents do not like to hand over responsibility to paid carers as this suggests that professionals know better and some parents are frustrated that this new professional knowledge may override any family knowledge of their child, disregarding their input. It may be that during case conferences or meetings about your child you find that you have been stereotyped – perceived as having a different agenda to the professionals involved, needs that contrast to those identified for your child and that you may be viewed as competing against your child for limited resources. There have been some reports that suggest that some professionals overstate differences in the needs and interests of parents and their child because of these stereotypes.

Another stereotype is that parents feel stressed and overburdened by having a child with ASD and therefore are not resourceful and able to experience uplifts and successes in life. As we have written at the beginning of this chapter on developing good relationships with professionals, there has also been a lot of interest and research into why some families suffer from more stress than others. This is why there are still professionals who suggest that you need a break from the daily grind or caring for your child.

Another stereotype is one held by some parents that the professional is the 'expert' and therefore we have the situation where the 'expert' is held in awe, gives instructions/makes decisions and the parents are passive in that they obey these instructions without any discussion. Sometimes this situation may be useful in that you need a short-term response to an emergency situation. However, beyond this short-term response, this perception can be damaging.

Jan, a speech and language therapist, tells us:

Working with parents can be very satisfying as they often put in total commitment. They can use us as support but can also be too protective and not let their son or daughter take risks in all areas of life. They see too many professionals and too much paperwork to complete with not enough action. As a professional I have to be careful to keep the language jargon free. Please communicate! Most services have limited resources and have to decide how best to use them. If we think a client is managing recommendations well, they will not be seen so often, releasing time to be spent with those having difficulties. It is incredibly frustrating to find on a routine review that problems have arisen but that we have not been informed about them. If we have made recommendations that aren't working we need to know so that we can make whatever changes are needed to help the client and the family. Waiting until our next visit to tell us of any problems is not helpful and delays any progress and benefits that could be made. We are not offended if recommendations do not work as planned. Please be honest; giving us duff information means we are likely to give duff advice.

Cath, a dietician says:

It is so frustrating to be seen as the enemy before we have even met the client of the family. A number of families refuse to have our input before we have even been involved. Another frustration is when families completely ignore professional recommendations. We have seen clients die when our guidelines have been ignored. Dysphagia (swallowing problems) guidelines, for example. This is something that is very hard for us when we know the difficulties and risks a client faces but the families do not accept our professional assessment. Why don't families engage in discussion with us about the recommendations rather than shut us out and risk potentially life threatening complications?

Advice for parents on what they should expect from the professionals they come into contact with

We like the following advice by Koegal *et al.* in 1996, which Tony Osgood (2004) recommends for behavioural specialists and paid care staff in relation to managing distressed behaviour:

Step 1 What good things has your child got going for them in their life?

Step 2 Increase these good things, introduce new good things.

Step 3 Make good things non-contingent (in other words don't withhold them as a punishment).

Step 4 Then come back to 'me' and talk about distressed behaviour in six months.

The four steps listed above are a good way for you to check to see whether you can do anything else to help your son/ daughter before a referral is made for professional help…and if you need help *please* ask for it and show the professional person who walks through your door the steps you have taken, the changes you have taken to 'walk in their shoes'.

Most families, including those who are managing self-sufficiently, value proactive visiting and a listening ear from professionals even though they may not need any more practical support. The following ideas are a guide to help you to inform professionals so that you can develop a relationship with the professional that gives you the information and support you need, with no stress.

- It is more important for you to believe that you are appreciated and valued rather than receive special services. To do this identify what type of help you require (i.e. list the resources you already have/need) and if possible list your views on them (such as why you think they may help/have helped). If you identify a service that is not available ask why. Some parents would appreciate the opportunity to contact support groups, some parents prefer to be left alone. Let the professional know which preference you have.

- Understanding about family problems from your perspective. To do this identify what type of help you require (i.e. list the problems you have or the problems you are predicting, such as the transition from one school to another) and if possible list your views on these, which scares you most, which one is more important.

- The extent to which family members wish to be involved can vary greatly. Do not assume that your family can or cannot help; find out about their time commitments and factors which need to be taken into account (such as work, school, holidays, other commitments). It can be disastrous to put pressure on family members or exploit them. Identify who can help you and when and communicate this to the professional who is visiting you. This helps foster a working partnership.

- It is important for you see the relevance of the information to your family or to your child. If you have difficulties seeing the relevance ask more questions or seek other opinions so that you can make informed decisions.

- Effective listening conveys interest and understanding by the professionals; remember to use the same skills (reflect upon what they have said to you, asked you to do and repeat back to them in your own words to clarify).

- Has the professional really offered you help? Can you see more opportunities for your child to achieve success or for you to experience an uplift? If this is the case say so; do not keep quiet.

- Leaflets mean parents can access information when they want to – ask if the professional has any or can send you relevant ones.

- Parents need staged help – not bombardment. If you find yourself distracted or that you are being given too much information ask the professional to stop and suggest that you meet another time.

- Continuity – ask if you will be seeing the same professional each time or a member of a team.

- Honesty is the best policy: just as you would like the professional to be honest with you, be honest with them. This may pre-empt situations where you could be judged as resistant to change, or where you experience negative emotions such as failure.

CHAPTER 6

Medical Issues

Medication

Medical management

> For many years now, learning disability psychiatrists have kept on prescribing stuff – some of which is good, some of which is not. Medication is the primary intervention for challenging behaviour in the UK. (Osgood 2004)

Medication may have its place but needs to be seen in the wider context of behaviour management for this vulnerable group. It is not nor should it be the total answer to behaviours we find difficult to manage. Indeed in a recent article published in the *Lancet* it was found that there was no difference in behaviours between those given a placebo and those given antipsychotic medication to control challenging behaviour. It concludes that medication should no longer be seen as the first option in the treatment of challenging behaviour.

There is an emerging school of thought that there is no need at all for medication, sometimes referred to as 'chemical cosh', 'chemical straitjacket' or 'chemical restraint'. However we believe if we take this view we are in danger of throwing out the baby with the bath water. The old adage 'medicine is an art rather than a science' is never truer than in the field of learning disability and people who are diagnosed ASD, because certain medications often work but we're not always sure why! This is because clinical trials take place on healthy adults and there is a dearth of good quality research concerning and involving adults with ASD and this needs to change. What happens far too frequently is that medication is used as the first and quite often only option and poly prescribing is common. A perception of medical management is that this implies that the doctor has the skills to identify and cure. The patient's role therefore once they have provided the doctor with the information required to make a diagnosis is to be passive and compliant with treatment. This perception clearly is unhelpful when looking at suitable interventions or approaches for your child. The medical profession now looks at the complex interaction of biological, psychological and social factors in the conditions they treat and medical students may now be taught the 'bio-psycho-social model or framework'. The priority is to identify the presence of additional mental and physical disorders which may be contributing to your child's distressed behaviour. They will also assess whether there is an underlying biomedical cause (in other words the cause of your child's disability, if known, may be affecting their behaviour.)

In the search for treatment for autism, there has been discussion in the last few years about the use of secretin, a substance approved by the American Food and Drug Administration (FDA) for a single dose normally given to aid in diagnosis of a gastrointestinal problem. In the United Kingdom the Medicines and Healthcare products Regulatory Agency (MHRA) licenses prescribed medication (www.mhra.gov.uk) and the National Institute for Health and Clinical Excellence (www.nice.org.uk) gives access to guidelines and information on medication. Some drugs are licensed in America and not the United Kingdom or vice versa because the manufacturers have not gone through the necessary licensing procedures. But we use the drug as 'custom and practice' as other countries have shown them to be helpful.

Anecdotal reports on secretin have shown improvement in autism symptoms, including sleep patterns, eye contact, language skills, and alertness. However, you should also be aware that several clinical trials conducted in the last few years have found no significant improvements in symptoms between patients who received secretin and those who received a placebo. This reminds us that medication may appear to work for some but not all.

Medical action therefore could be needed as part of an intervention. For example if your child is scratching their skin until it bleeds, a medical examination may indicate that the scratching is due to a skin disorder and prescribing a topical medication such as a cream or ointment may solve this problem. The medications prescribed (such as antipsychotic, antidepressants, anticonvulsants) are often used to treat distressed behaviours that keep the person with ASD from functioning more effectively at home or school. The medications used are those that have been developed to treat similar symptoms in other disorders. Many of these medications are prescribed 'off licence'. This means they have not been officially approved by the government watchdogs for use in children, but the doctor prescribes the medications if they feel that they are appropriate for your child. Further research needs to be done to ensure not only the efficacy but the safety of medications used in the treatment of children and adolescents. The British National Formulary (BNF) which can be accessed online (www.bnf.org. uk) lists most side effects from medication. The older the drug the more side effects the BNF know about. Another website that gives details of side effects is www.medicines.org.uk.

Medication management for distressed behaviours

Antipsychotic medications have been used to treat severe behavioural problems and have been available since the mid 1950s. These medications work by reducing the activity in the brain of the neurotransmitter dopamine. Research has identified that there are over 50 kinds of neurotransmitters in the brain and that a shortage or excess of specific neurotransmitters (such as dopramine or serotonin) may be the cause of anxiety, depression, ADHD, and mood disorders.

The medications that you may have read about are haloperidol (Haldol), thioridazine, fluphenazine, and chlorpromazine. Chlorpromazine was discovered in 1952. Haloperidol was found in more than one study to be more effective than a placebo in treating serious behavioural problems. However, haloperidol, while helpful for reducing symptoms of aggression, can also have adverse side effects, such as sedation, muscle stiffness, and abnormal movements.

Placebo-controlled studies of the newer 'atypical' antipsychotics are being conducted on children with autism. The first such study was on risperidone (Risperdal). Results of the eight-week study were reported in 2002 and showed that risperidone was effective and well tolerated for the treatment of severe behavioural problems in children with autism. The most common side effects were increased appetite, weight gain and sedation. Further long-term studies are needed to determine any long-term side effects. Other newer or atypical antipsychotics that have been studied recently are olanzapine (Zyprexa) which has been marketed as for use in emergencies and as a substitute for haloperidol. Unfortunately this drug can cause weight gain and in some cases has led to the person getting type 2 diabetes.

Medication management for anxiety and depression

Selective serotonin reuptake inhibitors (SSRIs) are the medications most often prescribed for symptoms of anxiety, depression, and/or obsessive-compulsive disorder (also known as OCD). The medications you may have read about that are SSRIs are: fluoxetine (Prozac), fluvoxamine (Luvox), sertraline (Zoloft), and clomipramine (Anafranil). Treatment with these medications can be associated with decreased frequency of repetitive, ritualistic behaviour and improvements in eye contact and social contacts. In the United States the FDA is studying and analyzing research to better understand how to use the SSRIs safely, effectively and using the lowest dose possible. In the United Kingdom fluoxetine (Prozac) was originally written about as the new wonder drug, as there was no weight gain and no anticholinergic side effects with this drug, then almost immediately had bad press. This was because this drug was overused, overprescribed and as we keep stating not all drugs suit everyone.

Medication management for seizures

Seizures (also called epilepsy) are found in one in four persons with ASD. They are treated with one or more of the anticonvulsants, such as carbamazepine (Tegretol), lamotrigine (Lamictal), topiramate (Topamax), and valproic acid (Depakote). The level of the medication in the blood should be monitored carefully and adjusted so that the least amount possible is used to be effective. This will require your child to have regular blood tests because the aim is to have the seizures controlled with just enough medication or there is a possibility that your child could have overdose effects. Carbamazepine and lamotrigne are anticonvulsants and mood stabilisers.

Medication management for inattention and hyperactivity

Stimulant medications such as methylphenidate (Ritalin), used safely and effectively in persons with Attention Deficit Hyperactivity Disorder, have also been prescribed for children with autism. These medications may decrease impulsivity and hyperactivity in some children.

Dietary interventions

There is a view that food allergies cause ASD and that an insufficiency of a specific vitamin or mineral may cause some symptoms. Please talk to your doctor (and/or dietician) if you share this view. This way if your child is eating a special diet, you will be sure that your child's nutritional status will be measured carefully. A diet that some parents have found was helpful is a gluten-free, casein-free diet. Gluten is a casein-like substance that is found in the seeds of various cereal plants – wheat, oat, rye, and barley. Casein is the principal protein in milk. Since gluten and milk are found in many of the foods we eat, following a gluten-free, casein-free diet is difficult and very restrictive, which could create more problems than you are trying to reduce. A supplement that some parents feel is beneficial for their child is Vitamin B6, taken with magnesium (which makes the vitamin effective). The result of research studies is mixed; some children respond positively, some negatively, some not at all or very little.

Long-term use of medication may affect nutritional status and your child's wellbeing. Not everyone experiences side effects but you do need to be aware of them and talk to your doctor about foods which may combat the unpleasant side effects. For example medication such as chlorpromazine, risperidone and amitriptyline can result in a craving for sugary foods. Low calorie snacks may help.

Sometimes it is also important to be aware of the effects of food on medication – this is because they can enhance or reduce the effects. Once again please talk to your doctor. An example is grapefruit which can cause an accumulation of the side effects of carbamazepine.

Medication management: what you can do

Your child with ASD may not respond in the same way to medications as typically developing children. It is important that you see a doctor, psychiatrist or nurse prescriber who has experience with children with autism. Your child should be monitored closely while taking any medication. The doctor will prescribe the lowest dose possible to be effective. Ask the doctor about any side effects the medication may have and keep a record of how your child responds to the medication. Your record should note positive responses as well as negative. It will be helpful to read the 'patient advice' that comes with your child's medication.

Linda says:

> Christopher was first offered medication by a paediatrician when he was five. He said 'Of course there's always haloperidol – but it's a bit fierce for a five year old.' This was in response to my enquiry about suggestions on how to deal with the fact that Christopher didn't sleep.
>
> When he was 15, a consultant psychiatrist very sensitively persuaded me that it was in Christopher's best interests to look at medication as an option to help him through what was proving to be a very difficult time in his

life – the transition to boarding school. He understood my concerns, discussed everything with us and agreed a treatment plan that he would personally closely monitor.

For me, the emotional impact of having to resort to medication was devastating. Our consultant handled my anger and my pain very sensitively. The medication did have a beneficial effect, as he had promised, and it did not make Christopher drowsy. It set him back on an even keel, his mood was stabilized and crucially it gave us an opportunity to work with him. We had taken our eye off the ball and now we had a lot of work to do to make sure that all the environmental changes and strategies could be put in place to help Christopher cope with his autism. The medication took the edge off the aggression; however, it was this combined with giving Christopher predictability, structure and a low arousal environment which enabled us all to have a decent quality of life.

In the ensuing years on occasions we came under intense pressure to increase the dose. The staff at his school wanted him to have three doses a day, adding in the extra one at lunch time as 'his behaviour is worse straight after lunch'. I pointed out that the deterioration in behaviour was probably due to having an hour's unstructured time at lunch break (notoriously bad for people with autism). We worked to ameliorate these unfavourable environmental factors and things changed for the better without any increase in medication.

Possibly as a result of long-term use of medication Christopher has developed motor and vocal tics and high anxiety levels. A locum psychiatrist again suggested haloperidol – this time to counteract the tics – without any thought of reducing the other medication. When we challenged this he said that Christopher would always need medication for aggression: sadly this unenlightened and unhelpful attitude is still common amongst professionals. A second opinion agreed with us that first the medication was no longer effective and that the increased anxiety and the motor tics could be side effects of long-term use. So began a long and slow withdrawal of the medication. It was not an easy option and there were times when we all questioned ourselves; however, Christopher is now less anxious and the aggression has not returned as was predicted.

Three years ago Linda became part of the guideline development group for the new UK national guidelines for the prescribing of medication for behavioural problems for people with learning disabilities and challenging behaviour. She was asked to join this group as a parent and also in her role of Family Services Manager with a regional autism charity. Family carers often feel under great pressure from professionals and might not feel able to challenge or question decisions. Although the guidelines are for those prescribing medication to adults with a learning disability the expectation is that the good practice indicated should also apply to those prescribing to children and young adults. By understanding what is expected of the professionals it may enable you to be fully involved in any decision making process.

Some of the main recommendations are as follows:

- Following a full assessment a treatment plan should be drawn up.

- The prescriber should ensure a physical examination and appropriate investigations have been carried out.

- The prescriber should discuss the treatment plan with the person and/or their family.

- The prescriber should allow the person and/or their

family to influence the decisions that are made and included in the treatment plan.

- The prescriber should clarify to the person and/or their family if the medication is prescribed outside their licensed indication. If this is the case, they should be told about the type and quality of evidence that is available to demonstrate effectiveness.

- The prescriber should discuss with the person and/or their family common and serious adverse events related to the treatment.

- The prescriber should ensure regular monitoring and follow-up assessments.

- Consideration for withdrawing medication and exploring non-medication management options should be ongoing.

Referrals to professionals/agencies

In the United Kingdom, distressed behaviours are the most common reasons for which people with a learning disability are referred to a psychiatrist. It is also usually a third party that makes this referral on your behalf – filling out a referral form where there may be specific words or labels (the criteria for acceptance or not to this service).

The difficulty we are faced with in this country and others is that we all like to label what we see – give it meaning – and it is this process that can lead to confusion such as the following words:

- special needs/complex needs

- challenging behaviour/violence/aggressive behaviour.

Do the words used make a difference? And will the label affect the service you may be offered? It is our experience that yes the words used by yourselves and professionals do matter and can make the difference between meeting criteria for acceptance to a service or not, receiving a benefit or a difference to acceptance within a specific group/community. This is sadly why the term challenging behaviour will not be phased out in the near future but we live in hope.

Take the word violence. The Oxford and Collins English Dictionaries define violence as:

- the unlawful use of force

- the exercise or an instance of physical force, usually effecting or intending to effect injuries, destruction

- powerful, untamed or devastating force.

The Royal College of Nursing defines violence directed towards staff as 'any incident in which a health professional experiences abuse, threat, fear or the application of force arising out of the course of their work' (RCN 1998).

At this stage you may be thinking of the behaviours your son or daughter displays and wondering whether you should be thinking about their behaviour in terms of violent behaviours...the problem is that the general public's understanding of violence is mixed up with fear and attitudes which may not be useful in your situation.

In the United Kingdom there has been a debate about whether there is a need to have a qualification in learning disabilities nursing; in fact few universities offer student nurses this course. The downside to this may be that fewer pre-registration student nurses studying adult, child or mental health nursing who are given any exposure to what a learning disability, what autism is, what distressed behaviour is and their only information may be a textbook aimed at student nurses. Some include references to caring for an individual with a learning disability but many do not. Very few general nursing skills textbooks have a section discussing challenging behaviour – but most devote a section/chapter to aggression/ violence and we can find none that specifically caution the reader from applying what they are reading to the individual with a learning disability and challenging behaviour (distressed behaviour).

Hospital appointments

If you are visiting hospital and you know your son/daughter may find this appointment/visit difficult, it may be that you could contact them beforehand (or this may be something that you could ask the professional involved with your family if you have one to do on your behalf).

It is worth in your letter/telephone call stating:

- that your son/daughter has a learning disability and describe what that means to them in as few words as possible

- describe their distressed behaviour (and that it is not violent/aggressive behaviour in the terms that they may know in their textbooks/policies)

- what you do to manage it

- situations that may trigger this behaviour

- warning signs

- what you would like from the hospital service (be reasonable here) – you may want to be shown to a quiet room to wait for your appointment, you may want the first or last appointment of the day to reduce waiting times, you may need to be waiting quietly in the car and be called to the appointment only when you can walk straight in, you may want all staff to ignore your son/daughter's behaviour (such as screaming, swearing). It could just be that you want the person reading your letter and the staff involved to realize that you do not want to 'queue jump' and that you are not a terrible parent with an unruly child, or a child that is attention seeking!

Clinical procedures where your child may have to be still for a period of time such as having a blood test

Perhaps your son or daughter needs a blood test and you are concerned about how they react to this. It is worth mentioning here that whilst many of the nurses you may meet will have expertise in how to hold your child for this procedure, many nurses do not. There is a lack of comprehensive guidelines, policies or training for both registered staff and student nurses in the United Kingdom (Shinnick and Valler-Jones 2005), which may be why the nurse will ask you to hold your child.

Clinical holding is also referred to as restraint, which is defined as the 'positive application of force with the intention of overpowering the child'. Andrea prefers to use the definition by Lambrenos and McArthur (2003): 'positioning a child so that a medical procedure can be carried out in a safe and controlled manner, wherever possible with the consent of the child and parent/carer'.

Andrea has done some research into this subject with colleagues from Birmingham City University and Stafford University. Her enquiries have shown that registered nurses have had little or no formal training post-qualification on clinical holding. Some techniques have been adapted from other disciplines or developed through necessity. Research undertaken by Robinson and Collier (1997) looked at why nurses felt that restraint or clinical holding was necessary. A main justification was the inability of the child to give consent and understand the process. It is the author's experience that this issue has particular relevance to children with a learning disability who are often viewed as having poor cognitive development and maturity.

If you find yourselves in this situation, you may find that the nurses will ask you to hold your child. If though you are unhappy to do this or the nurses/doctors suggest holding your child for the procedure ask if the procedure is necessary or needs to be done at this time especially if your son or daughter is becoming upset. It could be that a referral needs to be made to a specialist team (such as the community nurse, psychiatrist or play therapist who will advise you on coping strategies to help make this procedure less traumatic).

Andrea is involved with a group of professionals who are developing evidence-based guidelines that are relevant, acceptable and reliable and develop a network to share best practice with the ultimate aim of devising and implementing a standardized evidence-based programme that encompasses training needs, legislation, ethical issues, children's rights and identifies a pathway for safe and informed practice which responds to identified needs.

Chapter 7

Other Common Problems

Questions

This chapter looks at some of the issues that we have been asked about at various training courses.

Diagnosis

Many parents worry about when or even whether to tell their child that they have ASD. When a child is younger they may not know they are different and if they have a severe intellectual disability diagnosis, this may not ever be an issue for your child, but as a more able child who may have been diagnosed with Asperger Syndrome (AS) grows up they will start to notice that they are different from their peers; this can lead to low self-esteem and withdrawal.

We also know that understanding themselves is crucial for your child's long-term social and emotional development. Any explanation will need to be age appropriate. Tony Attwood in his excellent book *The Complete Guide to Asperger's Syndrome* (2007) recommends using stories where the heroes are children with ASD; this will help their self-esteem and let them see their diagnosis in a positive light. He describes a tool that he has devised and finds particularly useful called the 'attribute activity'. We love this idea as it is a family activity and is used to help the child start to understand themselves and their autism:

- Gather the family together in one room.

- Put a sheet of paper on the wall, one for each person, and divide the paper into two columns; put the headings 'qualities' and 'difficulties' at the top of each one.

- Mum or dad goes first and writes up the personal qualities and difficulties she or he feels they have and then asks other members of the family to add to this list. This can include their practical abilities, knowledge, personality and passions.

- This has to be carefully controlled and we need to make sure that there are more qualities than difficulties on all the lists.

- Another member of the family then has their go so as to help the child with ASD to understand the process.

- Because of their low self-esteem the child may need encouragement when it comes to doing their own list.

Tony Attwood then goes on to tell the child that scientists usually look for a pattern and when they find it they give it a name. He then talks about the work of Hans Asperger and looks at the child's qualities and difficulties and suggests they meet his criteria; he usually ends the session by saying, 'Congratulations, you have Asperger Syndrome.' He then explains that they are not mad, bad or defective but different, with different ways of thinking and with talents and qualities due to the AS as well as difficulties. Interestingly his experience is that this activity can be carried out by the parents of younger children but adolescents are more likely to accept the diagnosis from a clinician. This book is a great resource for any parent of a child with AS.

Managing anger

Helping our children understand their emotions and giving them strategies to enable them to control negative feelings is crucial for their long-term development. The link between a feeling, linking that to an emotion and being able to express that emotion does not come easily to our children.

Linda says:

> Whenever Christopher became upset we would try and guess what he was feeling and actually say to him 'Christopher's feeling sad?' and touch his tears. We did the same when he was happy but it took him years to respond in a meaningful way and only recently has he been able to connect it all together. Now when he is sad he will say 'What's the matter, Christopher, you sad?' to which we will always respond and try to see what the problem is.

Being able to manage anger is really important, and our low arousal approach will help toward your child being allowed to manage their own anger. There are also some great resources available for more able children. Kari Dunn Buron (2007) and colleagues have used their considerable experience in the area to produce some great materials. They found that children with ASD often respond to rating scales; as they point out scales are visual and concrete and work well with children with ASD. They use the idea of a child rating their feelings at any given time or situation; if they rate it as '1' it means they are feeling calm and happy, through to '5' which means they are in danger of losing control. Not only does it help the child identify their emotional state but it also helps you identify which situations they might find difficult. We know parents who have had success with these materials with young children as well as adolescents. Their *A '5' Could Make Me Lose Control!* we think is a great activity-based work book.

Sexuality and relationships

We may be able to teach our children the mechanics of sex but this needs to be set in the context of the much more complicated issue of relationships. There is no black and white when it comes to our relationships but rather a lot of grey, so teaching our children what is appropriate and safe can be incredibly difficult. But that does not mean that we can just bury our heads in the sand and hope it all goes away. For those of our children who have severe learning disabilities our main task is to keep them safe by being vigilant as to the actions of others, but for those more able children and young people who will be venturing out into the wider world, along with independence goes risk.

Sue Hatton and her colleagues at autism.west midlands carried out research at their school on how to develop an appropriate curriculum for their young people. They found that there were 'essential building blocks' that needed to be put in place for the young people to get a better understanding of sexuality and relationships. Sue has written an article explaining this idea and an information booklet written for staff, details of which can be found on the autism.west midlands website.

Another excellent resource came to Linda's attention while working in South Africa: *I'm Growing Up – Relationship and Sexuality Education for Young People With Autism Spectrum Disorders* by Rebecca Johns (2007). It is written for parents, carers and teachers to encourage them to see sexuality and relationships education as an integral part of the school curriculum and home life. It is aimed at younger children and, just like Sue Hatton, Rebecca Johns lays down a foundation on which to build children's knowledge. The message is it's never too early to start and the work can be carried on throughout their (and our) lives.

ASD and criminal justice system

We have looked at the importance of teaching our children about sex and relationships as part of their ongoing social and emotional development. We also know that their confusion around these areas of their lives can lead to them coming into contact with the criminal justice system (CJS). They are also vulnerable to becoming involved in other sorts of criminal activities, although it must be stressed that even though there are reports of people with ASD committing serious crimes, this does not mean they are more likely to commit crimes than other members of the general population; in fact they are just as likely to be the victims of crime. However, it is evident that the core difficulties experienced by individuals with an ASD can lead to their involvement in the CJS either by a lack of understanding and misinterpretation of their behaviours by others or by their own lack of understanding of themselves and social rules. Their core difficulties, including poor under-standing of social relationships, communication problems, deficits in ability to interpret other people's intentions and thoughts and feelings which can lead to a lack of empathy with others and difficulty in understanding the social rules can all lead to problems.

> Dominic's parents had told him he could have a girlfriend when he started college. On his first day he saw a girl he thought was pretty and went and sat beside her. Alarmed, she moved away from him; over the next few weeks he continually sought her out and tried to get close to her. Eventually he was excluded from the college for sexual harassment. Ghaziuddin (2005) asserts that because of their 'social naivety' an individual with ASD's behaviour may be misinterpreted as sexual harassment (p. 224).

> Carl saw a girl on the train station and he liked her 'because she smiled at me'. He came back the next morning and tried to give her one of his favourite train models. She declined his offer and he became more insistent and would try and greet her every morning with a new model. He was arrested on suspicion of stalking. Attwood (2007) says that individuals with ASD may have problems in understanding the difference between kindness and attraction.

> Jake loved cars and had been caught stealing one. It transpires that a gang of boys had encouraged him to take the car saying that they had spoken to the owner and that it was OK.

There is much evidence to suggest that because of their rigidity of thought individuals with ASD adhere well to rules and regulations, meaning they are arguably less likely to break the rules; however, they may not tolerate well someone else breaking the rules!

> Mary had been on the bus and someone was smoking. She approached him and told him it was against the rules. When he told her to 'get lost' she tried to take

his cigarettes away. In the ensuing tussle she pushed him and he fell against the window banging his head; she was charged with assault.

The British Institute for Brain Injured Children (BIBIC), who have along with others campaigned for training for the criminal justice service professional, give examples of young people with ASD being given ASBOs (Anti Social Behaviour Orders):

- 15-year-old boy with AS given an ASBO because neighbours complained he was 'staring' over their fence into their garden.

- 15-year-old boy identified with Tourette's Syndrome given an ASBO because of his swearing in public!

- 13-year-old girl with AS who had been swearing in the street (it turned out that there had been a heated argument between her parents and the neighbours and she had been copying the language used).

By not understanding the individual's problems, and making unreasonable demands for compliance to these orders, the system is often setting our children and young people up to fail.

The National Autistic Society have expressed concerns that the definition of anti-social behaviour is too vague. In particular, it is held that 'behaviour which causes or is likely to cause harassment, alarm, or distress' could describe some of the core behaviours of many individuals with autism.

There is evidence to suggest that individuals with learning disabilities are vulnerable with regard to interrogation processes. Indeed, Debbaudt (2002) asserts that when being interviewed by the police, the individual may mistake friendliness or politeness as a sign of friendship, and may confess to an offence they did not commit to make their new friend happy.

Where there is an obvious intellectual disability, individuals should have automatic access to an 'appropriate adult' who can make sure that they understand the process. Increasingly there are members of this scheme that have specific knowledge about autism and its affects. However in the case of people with autism spectrum disorders who are higher functioning, this can be problematic as the individual's apparent intelligence is measured by standardized tests which may belie their core difficulties in social interaction, communication and understanding of consequences of their actions.

Thankfully, over the past few years, some organizations championing the needs of people with an ASD have started to raise awareness amongst criminal justice system professionals. Linda was involved in probably the first project of its kind in the UK: autism.west midlands formed the first criminal justice system forum in 2004 which now has the support of the five police forces that cover the West Midlands region as well as the Crown Prosecution Service, youth offending teams and Law Society. We also know that this work is going on in the USA where Dennis Debbaudt, a serving police officer and father of a young man with ASD, campaigns with others to raise awareness, and he has written an excellent book on the subject. The National Autistic Society (NAS) is also campaigning at a national level.

One of the most practical solutions to this problem is to alert those professionals that they may be dealing with a young person with an ASD; to this end the carrying of a card explaining the individual's problem is becoming popular. The autism.west midlands 'Attention Card' is available free to anyone with an ASD. It has a space for an emergency phone number to contact and the logos of all the regional police forces appear on the front, making it easily recognizable to the police. Also a similar 'Alert Card' can be obtained from the NAS. Other regional autism charities have followed the autism.west midlands lead and produced their own cards along the same lines, as has Autism Cymru in Wales. Details of these organizations can be found in our resources section.

Helping your child

- Make sure your child carries a card which identifies them as having ASD (in the UK, these 'Autism Alert' cards are available from the NAS).

- Speak to your local police station and Community Support Officers if you think your child may be vulnerable in the community.

- Work with your child to help them understand potentially offending behaviours, using Social Stories™ and Comic Strip Conversations, etc.

As we said in the introduction an important element of our parent courses is learning safe physical intervention skills. These consist of 'breakaway techniques': skills which enable you to remove yourself from hair pulls, attempted bites, grabs, etc. It also includes showing parents a safe way to restrain someone if all other options have failed. You may have experienced quite serious physical aggression from your child and this can be devastating. These skills cannot be taught from a distance and although it is a standard training course for staff working with challenging behaviour, we also know that services are reluctant to teach the skills to parents. We would encourage anyone who is experiencing these problems to talk to their community nurse, clinical psychologist or psychiatrist, or it may be that you could talk to your local Carers Project as they may be able to arrange such a course locally.

CHAPTER 8

Looking After Your Health

In the introduction, we said that 'This is a practical, honest, no nonsense handbook which we hope will give you the confidence, skills and knowledge to manage challenging behaviours in a positive way. It will help you take a look at how you and your family live together.' We are proud of what we have written and hope that if you identify areas that you feel need to be changed, this book will give you ideas and strategies to effect that change. In this book we have touched on the issue of stress.

Our reaction to stress is a primitive response. It dates back thousands of years to when humans faced life-threatening dangers every day.

Nowadays demanding or new situations can still evoke this prehistoric reaction. But today it might be a telephone call from your child's school or an important meeting about your child. Why do our bodies react in this way?

What is our body's reaction?

- raised blood pressure

- increased heartbeat

- restricted blood flow to the skin

- reduced stomach activity, causing a feeling of 'butterflies'

- increased perspiration.

At the same time, the body can:

- release sugar and fat into the system

- reduce the efficiency of the immune system, so we fight infections less well.

No wonder we end up with colds, stomach problems, headaches and feel rotten.

Often, of course, it may seem we have no option but to carry on in a stressful situation. But it is still important to try to stand back and consider whether we can make changes. Some people seem to thrive on a hectic lifestyle. Others find quite small demands stressful. We are all unique in the way we respond to pressure. Clearly stress is not solely down to what happens to us but also the way we think.

Psychologists argue that different personalities react differently to stress. People called type-A personalities – who are more likely to rush, be competitive and be perfectionists – are more prone to stress. Type-B personalities – who are more easy-going – cope better with stress.

We all react differently under stress and so the initial health effects can vary. Typical symptoms may include:

physical changes	mental changes
headaches	feelings of panic or anxiety
stomach upsets or feeling sick	irritability
back pain	depression
trembling	poor concentration
sweating	feeling helpless
difficulties sleeping	lacking confidence
more colds or infections	not wanting to socialize

Most people experience these sorts of problems at stressful times in their lives. Nobody should feel embarrassed or guilty because their body is telling them to slow down or take a break.

Managing stress

The secret of managing stress is to look after yourself and, where possible, to remove some of the causes of stress. If you start to feel things are getting on top of you, give yourself some breathing space.

One way to manage stress is to take a day off work, domestic chores, family and everything else that puts pressure on you. Spend the day doing only relaxing things that make you feel good. However, we recognize that you may not be able to do this as who else could look after your child...if you can not take the day off, can you take an hour or two away from the family just to relax? It can make all the difference, reducing the threat to your wellbeing.

Some ways to cope with stress:

- Accept offers of practical help.

- Do one thing at a time – don't keep piling stress on stress.

- Know your own limits – don't be too competitive or expect too much of yourself.

- Talk to someone.

- Let off steam in a way that causes no harm (shout, scream or hit a pillow).

- Walk away from stressful situations.

- Try to spend time with people who are rewarding rather than critical and judgemental.

- Practise slow breathing using the lower part of the lungs.

- Use relaxation techniques.

- Use a method of focusing your emotions to stop any stressful thoughts (ignore any stressful thoughts; give yourself some positive self-talk – i.e. I can do this – and imagine or focus on happier images).

If you are feeling low or depressed, your doctor will be able to advise you on suitable options such as joining a group to talk about your feelings. Perhaps you may be referred to a community psychiatric nurse who has an expertise in therapeutic interventions, a knowledge of medications, diet and exercises that can help. One other important thing your doctor or nurse should do is take your blood pressure (which as we have said is a key indicator of your health). Your doctor is checking that the readings are in what is known as the 'normal range'. Readings outside this may indicate that you have hypertension (high blood pressure) or hypotension (low blood pressure).

Looking after your emotions (anxiety, depression and loss)

In this section we start with the assumption that anxiety and depression are normal responses to adverse conditions, particularly those involving loss (the grief or mourning you may have because your child has ASD, may not leave home and get married/have children, the grief you may feel if there is a genetic link to their condition or the devastation having a child with a disability may bring).

An emotion is a mood state that involves the following:

- a subjective experience

- a cognitive appraisal (how we interpret the experience based upon our knowledge and experience)

- our physiological state (this is a range of internal bodily responses)

- our behavioural response (such as crying, moving away)

- and affect (this is our mood or our feeling).

Anxiety

As an emotion this can be described in terms of:

- a subjective experience – exposure to new, strange, threatening or potentially uncontrollable situations

- a cognitive appraisal – perceived uncertainty about what is happening or how we should respond to this experience

- our physiological state – raised heart rate, sweaty palms, shaking, feeling sick, difficulty in breathing, insomnia (such as early waking and worrying)

- our behavioural response agitation – obsessive checking, avoiding situations likely to make you anxious, seeking help

- and affect – tense, nervous, worried.

Anxiety is a normal response to stress, which we have written about earlier in this chapter. We have also given you ideas about how to manage your stress, because if this emotion persists it can have a serious impact upon your quality of life. There are a number of options available to manage anxiety, including seeing your GP, being referred for counselling or being referred to psychology services. Medication does not cure anxiety, but can offer temporary respite from the feelings you are experiencing. There are several approaches used to treat anxiety including challenging any negative thoughts that you have which are causing you to feel anxious; or talking about your thoughts and fears to help you explore ways of feeling more confident about finding solutions to these problems. Please read the section on managing stress for more ideas.

Depression

As an emotion this can be described in terms of:

- a subjective experience – powerlessness in the face of life events or even life in general

- a cognitive appraisal – sense of hopelessness which may be accompanied by negative or suicidal thoughts

- our physiological state – fatigue, sluggishness, poor sleep pattern, loss of concentration, poor appetite with weight loss or weight gain, feeling ill

- our behavioural response – social withdrawal, inactivity, lack of self-care

- and affect – persistent low mood, general loss and interest in life.

It is normal to feel emotionally low when we experience a loss or things go wrong. However, whilst depression is common and most cases resolve themselves without intervention, occasionally you do need to access help from your GP. There is research that suggests that people who are depressed have little positive reinforcement (or pleasure) in their lives. If this rings true with you, it may help to look at how you can change this. Once again the suggestions we have included on how to manage stress may help.

Dealing with loss

Andrea visited a family where the mother was unable to tell a school friend that her son has Down's Syndrome. The mother thought her friend had guessed especially as he was now 26 years old and she had never shown her school friend any photos of him. An extreme case, but this mother was grieving for the child she never had and the conversations she could never have with her school friend. This mother tried to deny to her friend that anything was wrong.

It is important to 'work through' feelings of loss in your own way. For some this may be by talking about your emotions. For others it may be many years before you can work through your grieving. For others there is an acceptance that this is a normal state and, whilst painful, will be resolved through time, or by setting new goals for your child and family.

Looking after your back

Does your back hurt? Are you having to pick your child off the floor?

There are some simple preventative measures that you should consider – avoid what is known as a top heavy bend or a top heavy bend and twist…in other words do not reach down to pick anything up by keeping your legs straight or twist your body. Instead have your feet shoulder width apart and one foot more forward than the other for balance. Bend your knees and let your head lead all movement (in other words when you are picking something up look down, when you are ready to stand up look up). Exercise helps strengthen your back – such as yoga (and Wii Fit™).

If you do have back pain, go and see your doctor who can advise you on medications and exercises that may help.

Looking after your diet

The following recommendations for healthy eating are based on 'The Balance of Good Health' which is consistent with the government's tips for eating well:

- About a third of your meal should be starchy foods (pasta, rice, potatoes, wholemeal bread).

- Eat lots of vegetables and fruit.

- Eat more fish.

- Cut down on saturated fat and sugar (eat in small amounts and not too often).

- Eat less salt.

- Drink plenty of water.

- Get active and try to be a healthy weight.

- Don't skip breakfast.

And finally:

We hope you have found this book useful; our ultimate aim was to help you manage challenging or distressed behaviours in a positive way. Some parents we have come into contact with initially felt that their child would only learn if they were punished for their behaviour. We would never recommend this as an option; not only is it morally questionable but it is usually only effective in the short term and the response is born out of fear rather than necessarily understanding what they have done wrong. We hope you see that the approach we advocate is not the 'soft' option but rather a more effective and long-term answer to maintaining a positive relationship with your child.

Resources

All the following organizations have very good information, advice and resources for anyone caring for an individual with ASD.

Amicus
www.amicustheunion.org/pdf/stress-guide.pdf
The Amicus guide to stress including the symptoms of stress, stress and the law, the causes and consequences of stress, tackling stress and rehabilitation for stressed workers.

Autism Awareness Centre Inc. Canada
9331-151 Street
Edmonton, Alberta
Canada T5R 1K1
Email: vicki@autismawarenesscentre.org

Autism Cymru
National Office
6 Great Darkgate Street
Aberystwyth
Ceredigion
SY23 1DE
Tel: 01970 625 256
Email: sue@autismcymru.org
Website: www.awares.org

Autism Northern Ireland (PAPA)
Donard
Knockbracken Healthcare Park
Saintfield
Belfast
BT8 8BH
Tel: 0208 9040 1729
Email: info@autismni.org
Website: www.autismni.org

Autism Society of America
Website: www.autism-society.org

Autism South Africa (ASA)
Memorial Institute for Child Health and Development
Gate 13, Cnr Joubert Street Ext and Empire Road
Braamfontein. 2001
South Africa

PO Box 84209
Greenside, 2034
South Africa
Tel: +27 11 484 9909/23
Fax: +27 11 484 3171
Email: info@autismsouthafrica.org
Website: www.autismsouthafrica.org

Autism West Midlands
18 Highfield Road
Edgbaston
Birmingham
B15 3DU
Tel: 0121 450 7575 (Information
Service Helpline 10.00am – 2.00pm)
Email: info@autismwestmidlands.org.uk
Website: www.autismwestmidlands.org.
uk

**British Institute for Brain Injured
Children (BIBIC)**
Website www.bibic.org.uk

Contact a Family
209-211 City Road
London
EC1 1JN
Tel: 0207 7608 8700
Email: info@cafamily.org.uk
Website: www.cafamily.org.uk

MindTech Associates
www.mindtec.co.uk/stress-art
Several interesting articles on stress, a
free online stress test, an explanation of
how learning to breathe properly can
help you to control your stress, links
to books on stress and access to other
stress relief and control techniques.

National Autistic Society
393 City Road
London
EC1V 1NE
Tel: 020 7833 2299
Helpline: 0845 070 4004
Parent to Parent Support Line: 0800
9 520 520
Email: nas@nas.org.uk
Website: www.nas.org.uk

Sibs
www.sibs.org.uk
Support for brothers and sisters of
disabled children and adults.

Stressbusting
www.stressbusting.co.uk
Provides a wide range of information
about stress, has a range of articles on
how to cope with stress, alternative
therapies which may help, and a stressbusting forum.

Studio III Training Systems
Gay Street
Bath
Email: info@studio3.org
Website: www.studio3.org

The Scottish Society for Autism
Head Office
Hilton House
Alloa Business Park
Whins Road
Alloa
FK10 3SA
Tel: 01259 720 044
Email: autism@autism-in-scotland.
org.uk
Website: www.autism-in-scotland.
org.uk

Further Reading

The following list of books is just some of the ones we have found particularly useful.

Attfield, E. and Morgan, H. (2006) *Living with Autistic Spectrum Disorders – Guidance for Parents, Carers and Siblings.* London: Paul Chapman Publishing.

Attwood, T. (2007) *The Complete Guide to Asperger's Syndrome.* London: Jessica Kingsley Publishers.

Bogdashina, O. (2003) *Sensory Perceptual Issues in Autism and Asperger Syndrome: Different Sensory Experiences – Different Perceptual Worlds.* London: Jessica Kingsley Publishers.

Caldwell, P. (2008) *Crossing the Minefield – Establishing Safe Passage Through the Sensory Chaos of Autistic Spectrum Disorder.* Brighton: Pavilion Publishing (Brighton) Ltd.

Caldwell, P. with Horwood, J. (2008) *Using Intensive Interaction and Sensory Integration – A Handbook for Those who Support People with Severe Autistic Spectrum Disorder.* London: Jessica Kingsley Publishers.

Clements, J. (2005) *People with Autism Behaving Badly.* London: Jessica Kingsley Publishers.

Debbaudt, D. (2002) *Autism, Advocates and Law Enforcement Professionals.* London: Jessica Kingsley Publishers.

Dunn Buron, K. (2007) *A '5' Could Make Me Lose Control! An Activity Based Method for Evaluating and Supporting Highly Anxious Students.* Shawnee Mission (Kansas): Autism Asperger Publishing Co.

Dunn Buron, K. and Curtis, M. (2003) *The Incredible 5-Point Scale – Assisting Students with Autism Spectrum Disorders in Understanding Social Interactions and Controlling their Emotional Responses.* Shawnee Mission (Kansas): Autism Asperger Publishing Co.

Gray, C. (1994) *My Social Stories Book*™ (www.thegraycenter.org). London: Jessica Kingsley Publishers.

Gray, C. (1995) *Comic Strip Conversations.* Arlington: Future Education.

Hanbury, M. (2007) *Positive Behaviour Strategies to Support Children and Young People with Autism.* London: SAGE Publications Ltd.

Johns, R. (2007) *I'm Growing Up – Relationship and Sexuality Education for Young People with Autism Spectrum Disorders.* South Africa: Autism South Africa (ASA) – (available from National Autistic Society).

Nind, M. and Hewett, D. (2001) *A Practical Guide to Intensive Interaction.* Kidderminster: British Institute of Learning Disabilities.

Seach, D. (2007) *Interactive Play for Children with Autism.* Abingdon: Routledge.

Whitaker, P. (2001) *Challenging Behaviour and Autism – Making Sense – Making Progress (A Guide to Preventing and Managing Challenging Behaviour for Parents and Teachers).* London: The National Autistic Society.

References

Attwood, T. (2007) *The Complete Guide to Asperger's Syndrome.* London: Jessica Kingsley Publishers.

autism.west midlands website and fact sheets. www.autismwestmidlands.org.uk

Bogdashina, O. (2003) *Sensory Perceptual Issues in Autism and Asperger Syndrome: Different Sensory Experiences - Different Perceptual Worlds.* London: Jessica Kingsley Publishers.

Bogdashina, O. (2005) *Communication Issues in Autism and Asperger Syndrome.* London: Jessica Kingsley Publishers.

Bramble D. (1997) 'Rapid acting treatment for a common sleep problem.' *Developmental Medicine and Child Neurology 39,* 543-547.

Caldwell, P. with Horwood, J. (2008) *Using Intensive Interaction and Sensory Intergration–A Handbok for Those who Support People with Severe Autistic Spectrum Disorder.* London: Jessica Kingsley Publishers.

Carr, E.G., Horner, R.H., Turnbull, A.P., Marquis, J.G. *et al.* (1999) *Positive Behavior Support for People with Developmental Disabilities: A Research Synthesis.* Washington: AAMR.

Dagnan, D. (2007) *Thoughts About Challenging Behaviour.* dave.dagnan@cumbria.nhs.uk

Debbaudt, D. (2002) *Autism, Advocates, and Law Enforcement Professionals.* London: Jessica Kingsley Publishers.

Department of Health (2007) *Good Practice in Learning Disability Nursing.* London: DoH.

Donnellan, A.D. and Leary, M.R. (1995) *Movement Differences and Diversity in Autism/Mental Retardation.* Madison, WI: DRI Press.

Dunn Buron, K. (2007) *A '5' Could Make Me Lose Control!* Shawnee Mission, Kansas, IL: Autism Asperger Publishing Co. USA.

Emerson E. (1995) *Challenging Behaviour: Analysis and Intervention in People with Learning Disabilities.* Cambridge: Cambridge University Press.

Ghaziuddin, M. (2005) *Mental Health Aspects of Autism and Asperger Syndrome.* London: Jessica Kingsley Publishers.

Gray, C. (1994) *The New Social Stories™ Book.* Arlington: Future Horizons.

Jarvis, R. (2000) 'Professionals: a personal perspective from a parent.' *Community Connecting: Valuing People With Learning Disability 12,* January/February 2008, 29–30.

Johns, R. (2007) *I'm Growing Up – Relationship and Sexuality Education for Young People with Autism Spectrum Disorders.* South Africa: Autism South Africa.

Koegal, L.K., Koegal, R.L. and Dunlap, G. (1996) *Positive Behavioural Support: Including People with Difficult Behaviour in the Community.* Baltimore, MD: Paul H. Brookes Publishers. In T. Osgood (2004) *Suit You Sir? Challenging Behaviour in Learning Disability Services.* Canterbury: Tizard Centre, University of Kent, Canterbury.

Lambrenos, K. and McArthur, E. (2003) 'Introducing a clinical holding policy.' *Paediatric Nursing 15,* 4, May.

McDonnell, A.A. (in press) *Managing Aggressive Behaviour in Care Settings: The Use of Low Arousal Approaches.* Wiley.

Osgood, T. (2004) *Suit You Sir? Challenging Behaviour in Learning Disability Services.* Canterbury: Tizard Centre, University of Kent, Canterbury.

RCN (1998) *Dealing With Violence Against Nursing Staff: An RCN Guide for Nurses and Managers.* London: Royal College of Nursing.

Robinson, S. and Collier, J. (1997) 'Holding children still for procedures.' *Paediatric Nursing 9,* 4.

Sainsbury, C. (2000) *Martian in the Playground. Understanding the School Child with Asperger's Syndrome.* London: Lucky Duck Books.

Schopler, E. and Mesibov, G. (1994) *Behavioural Issues in Autism.* New York, NY: Plenum Press.

Shinnick, A. and Valler-Jones, T. (2005) 'Holding children for invasive procedures: preparing student nurses.' *Paediatric Nursing 17,* 5.

Wing, L. and Gould, J. (1979) 'Severe impairments of social interaction and associated malnormalities in children: epidemiology and classification.' *The Journal of Autism and Developmental Disorders 9,* 11–29.

Index